D1593658

Mahmoud Darwish

Mahmoud Darwish

The Poet's Art and His Nation

Khaled Mattawa

Syracuse University Press

For a listing of books published and distributed by Syracuse University Press,
visit www.SyracuseUniversityPress.syr.edu.

ISBN: 978-0-8156-3361-7 (cloth)   978-0-8156-5273-1 (e-book)

Library of Congress Cataloging-in-Publication Data

Mattawa, Khaled.
Mahmoud Darwish : the poet's art and his nation / Khaled Mattawa. — First edition.
         pages cm
Includes bibliographical references and index.
ISBN 978-0-8156-3361-7 (cloth : alk. paper) — ISBN 978-0-8156-5273-1 (ebook)
1. Darwish, Mahmud—Criticism and interpretation.   2. Politics and literature.
I. Title.
PJ7820.A7Z7389 2014
892.7'16—dc23   2014006798

Manufactured in the United States of America

For Halima, my mother.
For her bread and her coffee.

Khaled Mattawa was born in Benghazi, Libya, in 1964 and immigrated to the United States in 1979. He received an MFA in creative writing from Indiana University and a PhD from Duke University. Mattawa is the author of four books of poetry, *Tocqueville* (New Issues Press, 2010), *Amorisco* (Ausable Press, 2008), *Zodiac of Echoes* (Ausable Press, 2003) and *Ismailia Eclipse* (Sheep Meadow Press, 1996). He has translated nine books of contemporary Arabic poetry by Adonis, Saadi Youssef, Fadhil Al-Azzawi, Hatif Janabi, Maram Al-Massri, Joumana Haddad, Amjad Nasser, and Iman Mersal, and has coedited two anthologies of Arab-American literature. Mattawa's latest volume of poetry, *Tocqueville*, won the 2011 San Francisco Poetry Center Book Award and the Arab American National Book Award. His translation of Adonis's *Selected Poems* won the PEN USA Center annual poetry in translation prize. Mattawa's awards include the 2010 Academy of American Poets Fellowship Prize, a Ford/United States artist for 2011, the Alfred Hodder fellowship from Princeton University, a Guggenheim fellowship, an NEA translation grant, and three Pushcarts. He is an associate professor of Creative Writing at the University of Michigan.

Contents

Preface

One of the great privileges of my life was having the first Palestinian I met in Palestine be the poet Mahmoud Darwish. It was June 2000, and I had arrived as a Fulbright scholar to Palestine. The American embassy driver taking me to Ramallah spoke in broken English so quietly that I could never tell what he was saying or whether his native language was Hebrew, Arabic, or Russian. Along with us for part of the ride was an American military officer who said not a word and radiated an intense hostility that seemed to make the van go faster than it would have otherwise. I was relieved to arrive at last in Ramallah and to open the noisy iron gate of the Sakakini Center. I quickly climbed a short flight of stairs and tried to open the center's front door. When it did not open, someone shouted from inside, "You need the downstairs door." I said "thanks," and the voice replied with a casual "Marhaba!" (Welcome!) Just as I began to head back, I paused because something about the voice held me. Turning around, I quickly peered through the window to see who spoke. Indeed, it was Mahmoud Darwish sitting at a large, ornate, and rather neat desk; he was the first to welcome me into Palestine.

More importantly, of course, I want to credit Darwish for initiating me into poetry as I know and practice it. In

December 1988, in an Arab grocery store on Atlantic Avenue in Brooklyn, I found dusty copies of Mahmoud Darwish's early books among the sacks of dried goods, cassettes, coffee kettles, and prayer rugs. I had been writing for a couple of years by that point, but it had been only a few months since I allowed myself into poetry. That night, in my room, I read a little bit of Darwish, translated it into English, and went back to reading other books of poetry I had brought with me. In between reading and translating, I put down ideas for poems, and even a few lines of my own.

Translating Darwish as I read English verse, I received two floods of poetry: the poetry I longed to write and the language I wanted to write poetry in. I suspect that my writing mode remains positioned at this nexus of two desires, a braiding of lack and abundance. What struck me most about Darwish's poetry then was not its politics or its Palestinianness, but the fact that it satisfied my inner poetic ear and eye—the cadence of Arabic verse I'd inherited in my upbringing and the deep imagery I associated with modern verse. Darwish's was poetry I'd known before, but it was also poetry I was discovering anew.

My personal connections to Darwish are typical of his influence and legacy. Born in 1941, seven years before the *Nakba* (catastrophe), Mahmoud Darwish has guided millions to Palestine, including the Palestinians themselves. His poem "Identity Card," first recited in 1957 in a Nazareth movie house, was in essence the calling card that the Palestinians flung at their Israeli occupiers. Its impact on Palestinians and Arabs in general could not be exaggerated. Darwish's poems to Rita and his well-known "A Soldier Dreams of White Lilies" introduced the Israelis to the Palestinians and vice versa. Darwish instinctively knew that in order to assert the humanity of his people, he needed to likewise assert the humanity of his adversaries. Because he was committed to his art, Darwish knew that the road to his nation had to be demanding in order to be fulfilling and fulfilled.

Darwish's poems of exile after he left for Cairo in 1971, his post–Beirut poems of the mid-1980s, and his poems of the Oslo Accord period comprise a complex and varied meditation that is particular to the Palestinian saga of displacement and struggle. If he had written only those poems, he would easily be credited for composing a body of work that belongs among the twentieth century's best poetry.

There is hardly a moment in Palestinian history that Darwish's poetry has not treated. Coauthoring the Palestinian declaration of independence, chronicling the 1982 siege of Beirut, or remarking on cultural and political developments in Israel, Darwish and his lyrical voice can be found in masterful works of prose in addition to his poetry. No conversation among Palestinians or any presentation of themselves to the world occurs without alluding to his work. This is not to praise Darwish's genius, but rather to say that the Palestinian ethos was embodied in him because he worked tirelessly and continuously to attain this level of relevance and depth.

For decades, the Palestinian people were disparaged as their Zionist occupiers flooded the world with a contradictory myth of fragility, military genius, and cultural superiority. Now we can see that the Palestinians, whose dream of a nation-state is still under threat, have largely reversed the world's cultural perception of them. Who can now say, in the world's court of public opinion, that the Palestinians should be denied their dream? The myth of Israel as the sole democracy in the Middle East that had greened the desert is being continuously supplanted by the reality of Israel as a militarized state whose colonial-settler citizens are confiscating Palestinian lands daily. On the Palestinian side, even in Hamas-led Gaza, the Palestinians emerge mostly as civilians building a society where arts and culture have provided a more solid backbone than militancy. Precisely because of his impact on Palestinian artists and cultural activists around the world, Darwish's contribution to this element of the Palestinian identity is undeniable. As such, Darwish continues to provide a metonymic representation of Palestine. His poems express Palestinians' suffering as an occupied people, their longing for peace, the particularities of their relationship to the land and to one another, their feelings for their enemies, the anguish of their protracted exile, and their endurance through a history filled with disappointments.

This book is a humble effort that aims to demonstrate Darwish's own evolving approach to poetry and how his aesthetics have played a crucial role in shaping and maintaining Palestinian identity and culture through decades of warfare, attrition, exile, and land confiscation. Perhaps not surprisingly, we'll find that Darwish's work has changed widely over the years in response to historical developments and to personal circumstances. A young poet igniting resistance in occupied land, Darwish—in his first decade as a poet—also laid the groundwork for peace among the contestants. As he declared in "Identity Card," anger then and later would always have to be justified. Such justification was what poetry required. Even from the pits of Palestinian despair during the Beirut years, Darwish attempted to provide a mythology of honor and heroism. He may not have aesthetically succeeded, but the effort was noble nonetheless. In the decades of exile that followed, Darwish's projects grew in ambition and scope, as did his stylistic innovations. His books written from the mid-1980s to the late 1990s are arguably his best. The post–Oslo Accord years, beginning in 2000 until his death in 2008, saw Darwish in full command of his poetic skills. The poet was busy responding in verse to political developments, and he continued poetic projects that reached toward the philosophical even as he stood in the shadow of death.

By the time he passed in 2008, Darwish may have found peace that he was indeed wholly Palestine and wholly himself. The pressure on Darwish had been the requirement that he be the nation's poet, while he repeatedly insisted that Palestine be a nation worthy of poetry. The nation's endurance, therefore, lay in the capacity of its poetry to endure, to remain relevant as both rooted to its place of longing and in its transcendence of place as it reaches for the universal and the human to define itself. In that sense, Darwish is very much of and in Palestine. He perpetually welcomes readers to poetry and to Palestine, which he imagined as one and the same.

Acknowledgments

I am indebted to Srinivas Aravamudan, James Applewhite, Miriam Cooke, and Ian Baucom for their valuable insights on this manuscript. Warm gratitude goes to Mary Selden Evans for her enthusiasm for this book and to Deanna McCay for carrying it through to publication. Blessings to Issa Boullata, Steven Salaita, Fady Joudah, Terri DeYoung, and Reza Aslan for embracing this book. And, finally, boundless thanks to Megan Levad and Rachel Rosolina for your incisive copyediting.

*

Permission to reprint selected poetry and text from the following sources is gratefully acknowledged.

al-'Aili, Anas. "A Plant" in *Ḍuyūf al-nār al-dā'imūn: shu'arā' min Filasṭīn*, 7. Beirut: al-Mu'assasah al-'Arabīyah lil-Dirāsāt wa-al-Nashr.

al-Shaikh, Abdul-Rahim. 2006. July 3–7. "Fleeting Heterotopias: Troy, Andalusia, and the Whirling Darwish of Palestine." Unpublished paper presented at the Humanities Conference, University of Carthage. http://h06.cgpublisher.com/proposals/527/index_html#author-0

Darwish, Mahmoud. 2002. *Ḥalat ḥiṣar*. Beirut: Riyyāḍ al-Rā'yīs lil-Kutub wa-al-Nashr.

Darwish, Mahmoud. 2005. *al-'A'māl al-'ulā*. 3 vols. Beirut: Riyyāḍ al-Rā'yīslil-Kutub wa-al-Nashr.

Darwish, Mahmoud. 2006. *al-'A'māl al-jadīdah*. Beirut: Riyyāḍ al-Rā'yīs lil-Kutub wa-al-Nashr.

Zaqtan, Ghassan. 1999. "Akthhāriyāt al-hāmish." In *Duyū-fal-nār al-dā'imūn: shu'arā'min Filastīn*, 135–136, Beirut: 'al-Mu'assasah al-'Arabīyah lil-Dirāsāt wa-al-Nashr.

Note on Translations and Transliteration

All translations of Darwish's work and of all the Arabic references cited in this book are mine. For transliterating Arabic words and titles I have used the Library of Congress Arabic transliteration system.

Mahmoud Darwish

1

An Introduction

Perennial Tensions

Unlike Rabindranath Tagore, Derek Walcott, Aimee Cesaire, and Leopold Senghor, poets whose colonized nations gained independence in the second half of the twentieth century, Palestinian poet Mahmoud Darwish had no such fortune to accompany his similarly prodigious literary output and reputation. Darwish's career began and ended under Israeli occupation: the newly formed Israeli Defense Forces razed his home village in the Galilee in 1948, and Israeli settlements now encircle his burial site in Ramallah.

Darwish wrote one of his last books, *Ḥalat ḥiṣar* (*State of Siege*), in 2002 during a series of lengthy sieges of Ramallah, the de facto capital of Palestine. In *State of Siege*, Darwish revisits his earlier poetry and, at times, imagines being interrogated by the people he attempted to portray in his earlier works. The siege of 2002 evokes the soldiers who kept him under house arrest in the 1960s, as well as the 1982 Israeli siege of Beirut, where the poet lived under threat of death or capture by the Israelis. Darwish notes with sober irony how he and his people, more than ever, must "nurture hope" (2006, 117) as they continue to exist "within time's shot range,"

(177) facing a new generation of soldiers—the descendants of those who had imprisoned him decades before in Haifa.

Many critics acknowledge that Darwish's achievement can be said to have been, in John Bailey's words, the creation of a poetry that is "wholly contingent and yet makes of that very circumstance its own power" (2005, 373). Darwish acknowledges that confrontation with the Israeli occupier who threatens the lives of all Palestinians has been a constant presence in his life—a source of poetic energy as well as an impediment to poetic creation. "My early interest in poetry developed with my realization that I am a victim of some form of military and political aggression," he states (Darwish 1971, 244). Yet writing poetry without any references to the Palestinian issue, poetry "that focuses and fascinates the reader's mind" (377) without the pressures of the Palestinian contingency, has been one of Darwish's lifelong aims.

This tension between being a spokesman for his people and a private lyrical poet began to preoccupy Darwish very early in his career. Torn between his deep commitment to lyrical discovery and his desire to assist in the welfare of his people, the young Darwish considered himself "made up of two contradictory personalities" (1971, 250). "How can I combine my love for a girl and my association with the public cause?" (250) he wondered. Perhaps the central irony of *State of Siege* is that the poet was compelled forty-five years after "Identity Card" to write yet again about a confrontation with Israeli soldiers. *State of Siege* was published after *Sareer al-Ghariba* (*The Stranger's Bed*, 1996) and *Jidariya* (*Mural*, 2000)—two successive volumes that include no direct mention of or allusions to Palestine—during a period in which the poet seemed to at last have found his universal subject matter and poetic voice, having succeeded in making "a passage from the relative to the absolute" (Darwish 1999b, 81). This irreconcilable strain between poetry of external or political contingency and the dream of "universal" noncontingent poetry can be detected very early in Darwish's career. Addressing these concerns, Darwish, in his early poem "Ila al-qari'" ("To the Reader"), published in 1964, apologizes for writing about the difficult political conditions in which he lives, conditions that have driven him to anger. The assumption is that anger does not belong in poetry, or that political anger—and politics in general—would not have been part of his poetry, had he a choice in the matter.

"To the Reader"

Black irises in my heart
    and on my lips . . . flame.
From what forest did you come to me
    O crosses of anger?

I have allied myself to sorrows,
    I have shaken hands with banishment and hunger.
My hands are anger,
my mouth is anger
the blood of my arteries a juice of anger.
O my reader
    do not ask me to whisper,
    do not expect musical delight.

This is my suffering,
    a wild shot in the sand
    and another to the clouds.

My fate is my anger
and all fire starts out in anger. (2005, 15)

Where did this anger come from, the poet asks, and why was he burdened with it? These questions suggest that the poet was once in a state that precluded anger, and that anger is not his ordinary nature. We as readers, however, wonder when that peaceful state could have existed for Darwish and his countrymen between 1948 and the time of the poem's writing. Perhaps we are doing the poem injustice by assuming a close proximity between Darwish and the speaker of this poem. Yet the poet had already announced that he is one of the cooped-up Palestinians living in the state of Israel by titling his very first volume 'Aasafir bila Ajniha (Birds without Wings, 1961). He shortly thereafter published a volume titled "A Lover from Palestine," declaring himself a lover of the nation whose name was legally banned in the state of Israel. Readers are aware that the poet is a Palestinian who has begun to write after being exposed to decades of angry Palestinian poetry preoccupied with the travails of the homeland under British colonial rule and Zionist neocolonialism. Why would we not expect the poet to be angry?

It seems clear the young Darwish is up to something different with this apology to the reader. Until that point, no such precaution was heard or deemed necessary in twentieth-century Palestinian poetry. We are left to wonder what place the poet wishes to carve out for himself by bemoaning his unwanted anger. He declares that he would rather offer the reader some whispers, as expected of an amorous young poet, and some musical delight, suggesting that he wants to write different types of poems. Providing this apology, the poet acknowledges the reader's desire for placid poetry, that such a desire is proper, and that perhaps love poetry—full of positive emotions, serene meditations, and lyricism—is what poetry ought to be. Darwish, therefore, apologizes for having to write poetry that does not fulfill his reader's legitimate expectations.

Let's now turn our attention to the reader young Darwish anticipates, and to whom he feels he has to justify not only his anger but also the timbre and content of his future poetry. Would Darwish's fellow Palestinians object to his anger? Would his fellow Arab readers not understand his anger? Clearly not. By the time Darwish was writing, literature of commitment—*Adab al-Iltizam* (which I will discuss in more detail)—had become firmly established in Arab letters outside of Palestine/Israel. And within Palestinian literature, Darwish was part of the third generation of twentieth-century Palestinian poets whose careers were sparked in response to the British, and later Zionist, occupation of their land. So why then is our poet concerned, even apologetic, about being angry?

The issue goes beyond one poet's sensibility as it pertains to the particulars of the collective trauma experienced by the Palestinians. Here Darwish is speaking as a single self, but as with much of his work, that self-voicing is quickly embraced and claimed by other Palestinians. Darwish seems to argue that anger has no place in poetry, that poetry should offer the intimacy of whispers rendered with the consoling pleasures of music. Darwish knows this and announces his sadness that he cannot offer the reader either. But again, if Palestinians and other Arab readers expect no tame love poetry from Darwish and will willingly grant his anger license to sound itself, to whom is Darwish speaking then?

Couched in apology and sincerity, the poem is not without a degree of coyness. The poet apologizes for his anger even as he forcefully expresses it. The poem is short enough that it can stand being whispered, and at the same time it loudly states the poet's intention and dilemma. Also, the poet is clearly being ironic when he tells us not to expect musical delight, yet the poem is precisely measured and exquisitely rhymed. The point to which we ought to pay attention—and it is one that Darwish would bring up again and again through his career—is the poet's desire to write poems that do not arise from a fateful anger or, later, exile, siege, and betrayal. Darwish repeatedly expressed his longing to write poetry that goes beyond the ontological state of his existence, or the perpetual "madness of being Palestinian" (Darwish 1985, 38).

During the 1990s, several literary critics in the Arab world celebrated Darwish's success in extricating himself from the details of the Palestinian problems. Critic Fakhri Saleh delights in the fact that "Darwish has been able to draw lyric condensation that addresses the universal existential tensions of our postmodern times from the specifics of his experiences" (Saleh 1999, 49). Salma Khadra Jayyusi (1992), the leading canon-maker of Palestinian literature, judges Darwish's success mainly on his ability to transcend the political expediency of his earlier work and by his submersion into aesthetic experiments while remaining dedicated to the Palestinian cause (61–65). By the time Darwish published *Sareer al-Ghariba* (1996) and *Jidariya* (2000), he had been firmly established as the national poet of Palestine for three decades. The Palestinian political situation during the brief Oslo Accord years allowed for experimentation, and he, as a poet tied to the mission of national spokesmanship, felt he had a longer leash, permitting him to explore more freely. Several critics noted that Darwish had earned this phase of personal expression having given his Palestinian, and indeed all Arab, audiences so much over the decades (Bayḍūn 1999; al-'Usṭā 2001; and 'Abdulmutalib 1998).

One of the early gifts Darwish offered his Arab and Palestinian audience is the 1964 poem "Identity Card," which closes the volume *Awraq al-zeitoun* (*Olive Leaves*), in which the poem "To the Reader" also appeared. "Biṭaqat hawiyah" ("Identity Card") has been a fan favorite throughout the Arab world, one that audiences frequently asked Darwish to read before thousands of listeners at his recitations. The poem was made into a popular song and has been an unofficial Arab nationalist anthem for decades. Yet it is one that Darwish never read in public after leaving Israel/Palestine in 1971.

> Write it down!
> I am an Arab
> and my identity card is number fifty thousand.
> I have eight children
> and the ninth is due after summer.
> Does this anger you?

> Write it down!
> I am an Arab
> employed with fellow workers at a quarry.
> I have eight children.
> I earn their bread,
> clothes and books
> out of these rocks.
> I do not beg for charity at your doors.

Nor do I kneel
    on your marble floor.
    So does this anger you?

Write it down!
I am an Arab.
I am a name without a title,
patient in a country
where people live on furor or rage.
    My roots
    were entrenched before the birth of time
    and before the opening of the eras,
    before the pines and the olive trees
    and before the grasses grew.
My father comes from the family of the plow
    not from a privileged clan.
And my grandfather, a farmer,
    not well-bred or well-born,
taught me to be proud
before he taught me how to read.
    And my house is like a watchman's hut
    made of branches and cane.
    Are you satisfied with my status?
    I am without a title, just a name!

Write it down!
I am an Arab,
hair color, black as coal,
eyes brown.
Features:
    an 'iqal on my head tied around a kaffiyah,
a hand solid as a stone
    that scratches whoever touches it.

And my address:
  a weaponless village, forgotten,
  its streets too without names,
  all its men are in the quarry or the fields.
Does this anger you?

Write it down!
I am an Arab.
You have stolen my ancestors' orchards,
  the land I farmed
  with my children.
  You left us nothing
  except for these rocks.
  Will your State take them too
  as it's been said?!
So Now!
  Record at the top of the first page:
  I do not hate people
  nor do I steal.
  But if I become hungry
  I will eat my robber's flesh.
Beware then, beware of my hunger
  and my anger! (2005, 80–84)

Nothing in this poem diverges from Darwish's consistent message as a poet and spokesman for the Palestinian people. The poem's speaker, whose life details bear a remarkable resemblance to Darwish's own father, was expelled from his village, lost his farm, ended up working in a quarry, and fathered eight children. The angry speaker tells his story under occupation, how he has suffered patiently and remained proud despite the cruel hand the occupation has brought upon him. But now he draws a red line: he will not beg from the one who stole his land, and he will fight his usurper to fend off hunger; indeed, he will turn into a cannibal if need be. The speaker's last words, "Beware of my hunger / and my anger," irrevocably intertwined these two conditions. This poem provides a rational basis for the speaker's rage that resonates effectively with the references to anger in "To the Reader."

Why then has Darwish refused to recite the poem in public since he left Palestine/Israel, when it still encompasses his political stance and audiences around the Arab world plea for it? During one packed recitation in Beirut, a member of the audience kept saying "Write it down, / I am an Arab," asking that Darwish read the poem. Fed up with the repeated request, Darwish shot back at the listener, "Write it down yourself!" and went on to read a different poem (al-Sayyid 2008, 7). According to Darwish, the circumstances sparking the poem occurred when he was placed under partial house arrest in Haifa in the mid-1960s. He had been tried in court for a poem he published in 1965 (Snir 2008). The judge placed him under probation with the stipulation that Darwish could not leave his residence after sunset and that he sign in at the police station every day (al-Naqqāsh 1971).

"'Write it down: I am Arab!' I said that to a government official," Darwish explained. "I said it in Hebrew to provoke him, but when I said it in Arabic (in the poem) the Arab audience in Nazareth was electrified" (Darwish 2007a, 180). The poem, a dramatic monologue addressed to Darwish's detainers, continues as a translation of what Darwish would have said to the Israeli policemen in Hebrew. The audience was electrified because the poem succeeded in expressing in Arabic a private conversation that each humiliated Palestinian had experienced while facing Israeli officials and soldiers. Darwish turned private anguish into a public testament, evoking a collective feeling that broke down the barriers between I and We and between the poet and his audience. "Identity Card" was written within the first decade of the state of Israel, a time when the Israelis did not recognize the Palestinians as a nationality and the words *Palestine* and *Palestinian* were never mentioned in public. Palestinians who lived within the border of the state of Israel were merely Arabs. Darwish's translation and placement of expressions uttered in Hebrew into a poem written in Arabic made the private moment public and turned humiliation on its head. Palestinians living in Israel, beginning with the audience in Nazareth who asked to hear the poem repeated six times, identified with this reversal as a way to turn *Arab* from a derogatory term into a declaration of dignified humanity before the Israelis, who confiscated their lands and officially designated them third-class citizens.

Outside of Palestine/Israel, the refrain of the poem— "Write it down, / I am an Arab"—took on a different resonance, devoid of the specific context in which Darwish wrote the poem. "Write it down, / I am an Arab!" became a battle cry throughout the Arab world, and the poem became an anthem expressing Arab national pride and even chauvinism, as opposed to the defiance of subjugation and racism that the poet had meant it to be. Darwish explains, "the Jews call the Palestinian an Arab, and so I shouted in my torturer's face 'Write it down, I am an Arab!' Does it make sense then for me to stand before a hundred million Arabs saying 'I am an Arab'? I'll not read the poem" (al-Qaissī 2008, 13).

I bring up the history of Darwish's relation to "Identity Card" and his Arab audiences' claim upon it to point out his awareness of the contingent circumstances surrounding his poems. As opposed to his desire for "universal" noncontingent poems, here we see him insist that poems do target different audiences and serve as specific rhetorical gestures or even as political messages that should not be taken out of their historical context. In other words, poems do not necessarily have "universal" messages, because they emerge during different contingencies with different interlocutors.

To understand Darwish's career as a major search for poetic agency, this study outlines the evolution of Darwish's poetry, keeping in mind these two contending forces, or rather these two definitions of the role of poetry as a means toward agency, while operating within it. And though it is difficult to accept the polarities Darwish sets between engagement and private contemplation, love and political struggle, the expedient and the enduring, the relative and the absolute, what is remarkable is the degree to which Darwish managed to remain present as a discourse-maker in the Palestinian context, building bridges between these polarities for maximal agency. Darwish's discourse-making efforts manifest themselves in essays, interviews, and poetry.

The evolution of Darwish's poetry constitutes a struggle to preserve the poet's presence within political deliberations and to maintain and develop the aesthetic pursuit that grants the poet the degree of independence upon which his relevance as a discourse-maker depends. Darwish's poetry kept up with his various personal displacements and political affiliations. He redefined his role as a poet through his compositional practice, and his attempts to bridge the tension "between ethics and esthetics" (Darwish 1999a, 19) have helped shape the Palestinian national discourse and define the parameters and priorities of Palestinian identity formation.

2

The Poet and the National Literature

See
p. x.

Darwish was born on March 13, 1942, in the Palestinian village of Birwa, while it was still under British mandate. When he was six years old, the Israeli army occupied and then destroyed Birwa and over 400 other Palestinian villages. Darwish's family fled to Lebanon in 1948, then crossed the border back home a year later, settling in Dayr-al-Asad and then in al-Jadeeda, near where their village Birwa had been. Darwish and his family became internal refugees living under Israeli military rule, legally classified as "present-absentee aliens." Darwish recalls how his teachers in the Arab school he attended had to hide him from Israeli education officers who insisted that only Arab Israeli citizens could attend such a school. Darwish was never allowed to become an Israeli citizen; nonetheless, he and other Palestinians were very active in the Israeli communist circles, first with MAKI (the Communist Party of Israel) and later with Rakah (the Israeli Communist Party), which was the only Israeli party that accepted Palestinian/Israeli Arab members. After completing high school—he could not afford and would not have been allowed to enroll in an Israeli university—Darwish began to write for Arabic-language Communist newspapers and became a renowned figure for his articles and his poetry, often reciting to packed houses. Before leaving Israel in 1970, Darwish was imprisoned several times for reciting his poetry and traveling inside Israel without a permit. He was jailed five times and was subjected to long spells of house arrest, during which he was required to register daily at a police station in Haifa.

In 1970, Darwish was allowed to leave Israel as part of an Israeli Communist Party delegation attending a conference in Moscow, where he accepted a university scholarship. In 1971, he surprised his Palestinian colleagues at Rakah by arriving in Cairo, where he accepted an invitation to work as a journalist in Egypt's leading newspaper *Al-Ahram*; there he shared an office with future–Nobel laureate Naguib Mahfouz. Two years later, Darwish moved to Beirut to work at the Palestinian Liberation Organization's (PLO) Center of Palestine Studies, became fully involved in the PLO, and became part of the resistance to Israeli occupation of Palestinian territories.

He remained in Beirut through the 1982 Israeli occupation of the city, fleeing first to Tunis to continue working as part of the PLO's cultural apparatus, and then to Paris, where he edited *Al-Karmal*, the leading Palestinian cultural and literary review. In 1987, PLO chairman Yasser Arafat recruited Darwish to write the Palestinian Declaration of Independence, with Edward Said editing and supervising the English translation. Released at a momentous meeting of the Palestinian National Assembly, convened in Algiers in November of that year, the declaration laid the ground for a future Palestinian state that would exist in peace with Israel, based in territories occupied by Israel in 1967.

In 1993, Darwish resigned from all official affiliations with the PLO and the Palestinian Authority, headed by

Arafat, in protest of the signing of the Oslo Accords. He returned to Palestine in 1995 and devoted himself to his writing and to editing the *Al-Karmal*, which was supported by the Palestinian ministry of culture. Darwish lived between Ramallah and Amman, Jordan, until his death in August 2008. He died of complications following heart surgery. Darwish published twenty-five books of poems (one was published posthumously in 2009), five books of experimental writing, and several collections of essays. His work has been translated into more than two dozen languages. Darwish won a number of international awards, including the Lenin Peace Prize in 1983 (USSR), the Knight of the Order of Arts and Letters in 1993 (France), the Lannan Foundation Prize for Cultural Freedom in 2001 (USA), the 2004 Prince Claus award (the Netherlands), the Oweiss Prize in 2005 (United Arab Emirates), and the Arab Poetry Prize in 2006 (Egypt). Darwish's experiences as a Palestinian whose "array of displacements" (Nassar and Rahman 2008, 1) ran the gamut of Palestinian suffering made him a symbol of the Palestinians' cause and survival.

The Poet and Palestinian Literature

A Context

Historians of Palestinian literature agree that it was a minor component within the larger body of Arab literary work (see Jayyusi 1977, 1992; Kanafani 1966; al-Khaṭīb 1968; al-Naqqāsh 1971; and Sulaiman 1984). Palestine's best-known poets of the first half of the twentieth century, such as Ibrahim Ṭuqan (1905–1941), Abu Salma (originally 'Abd al-Karim al-Karmi, 1906–1980), and 'Abdulraḥim Mahmoud (1913–1948), never rose to become major poets in the Arab world, but they received some recognition after the 1948 Nakba. Though it houses the Haram al-Sharif, the third holiest site of Islam, Palestine itself "has never been the home of any central political authority and had not princes or patrons of art to help and encourage poets and writers" (Jayyusi 1992, 35). Palestinian youth seeking education traveled to Beirut and Cairo, as well as other world capitals, before and after the creation of Israel, and "many of the Palestinian talents that flourished before 1948 had lived and usually studied outside Palestine" (Jayyusi 1992, 6). Jayyusi (1992) explains that "although Palestinians were highly appreciative of culture and had quickly developed a modern educational system in the [second half] of the twentieth century, Palestine had, prior to the 1948 disaster, remained less affected by the literary currents blowing across the Arab world and had never been a center for the more innovative trends in other Arab countries in the vicinity of Palestine" (6).

Modern prose fiction fared rather badly in Palestine before 1948 and continued to struggle for a place in Palestinian literature. The entrenched position poetry held as the main literary genre of the region in combination with Palestine's political crisis fostered an atmosphere averse to experimentation. This is not say that the country lacked literary output. In fact, Palestinian poets were highly engaged with political and social developments in their country, especially after the Balfour Declaration of 1917, the British mandate in 1922, and from the 1936 revolt until the 1948 war.

Critics al-Naqqāsh, Mustafa, and Abū Shāwir argue that the years following the 1948 Nakba, which brought on the establishment of the state of Israel and the expulsion of hundreds of thousands of Palestinians from their ancestral villages, shocked Palestinian writers into "stunned bewilderment" (Jayyusi 1992, 18), driving many to silence for a few years. Palestinian literature began to reemerge after shock turned to anger at the agonies of Israeli political oppression, legal discrimination, and land confiscation. Palestinians inside Israel, like Darwish, were also buoyed by real transformations in the Arab world, such as the Egyptian Revolution of 1952, led by Gamal Abdul Nasser and the Suez Crisis of 1956; the beginning of the Algerian War in 1956; the unification of Egypt and Syria in 1958; and the nationalist revolution in Iraq that toppled a pro-Western monarchy, also in 1958. Critic Khalid Ali Mustafa (1978) notes that early on, Palestinian poets inside Israel resisted poetic innovations that had been taken up in the major Arab capitals, such as the modern *taf'ila* poetry. They stuck to the classical prosodic practice that mandated the use of a constant metrical pattern and a single rhyme scheme. Feeling "isolated, desiring to escape their reality, and seeking solace in poetry they were familiar with" (Mustafa 1978, 215), poets of the generation that preceded Darwish's employed diction that drew largely from the established classical and neoclassical repertoire.

Hardly any Palestinian prose fiction was written inside Israel/Palestine in the first decade after the Nakba. Palestinian writers in the diaspora, however, had a better chance of following up with developments emerging in other Arab regions. It was they who produced the first modern Palestinian short stories and novels, as represented in the work of Ghassan Kanafani, Samira 'Azzam, and Jabra Jabra. The diaspora poets such as Salma Khadra Jayyusi and Tawfiq

Sayyigh contributed to the revolutionary modernization of Arabic poetry in the 1950s.

The disjuncture in Palestinian literature between that written inside of Israel and outside of it (mainly Lebanon and Syria) occurred due to an effective blockade that the state of Israel enforced on its Palestinian Arab citizens. Amal Jamal explains that "The Arabic sphere between 1948 and 1967 was quite restricted" (Jamal 2009, 62). She adds:

> Limitations on freedom of expression suppressed voices that might have expressed the views and attitudes of the Arab minority . . . The military government did not tolerate any Arab political organization that propagated the Palestinian affiliation of the Arab minority or criticized the Israeli discrimination policies on the ground. Arab citizens of the state did not enjoy the freedom of expression that characterized the Jewish public, and so Arab publications issued by Arabs faced major distribution difficulties and were forcefully closed when they challenged the limits set for them by the military government. (62)

Qahwajī (1972, 281) reports that there was not a single public library in all the Arab cities or villages. A ban on Arab-owned presses and independent Arab publications went on for two decades, thus ensuring that Palestinians inside the state of Israel, like Darwish, were cut off from their Arab neighbors and from other Palestinians living there (Qahwajī 1972, 287–90).

A mutually imposed trade embargo between Israel and the Arab countries also denied Palestinians access to publications from the Arab world. Al-Naqqāsh notes that from 1948 to 1968, only sixty-four books in Israel were printed in Arabic, some of which were written by Arabic-speaking Jewish Zionists (1971, 32). Furthermore, the Israeli state denied the Arab population autonomy in running their educational affairs and underfunded this sector to "delay the emergence of political organization and movements" (Mar'i 1978, 5) among the Palestinians. Untrained teachers, who at times were perceived as agents of Israeli military (19), ran Palestinian schools. They were provided with only a limited curriculum that made no "mention of the Arab nationality or culture" (79). The curriculum, states Mar'i, made it appear "as though Arab literature is valueless, at least according to the [educational] planner's intentions. Jewish literature, on the other hand, appears quite valuable" (79). Serious learning in the sciences was done only in Hebrew, a language not all Palestinians could easily attain fully in their segregated schools. In sum, for the years between 1948 and 1967, Palestinians in Israel, most of whom no longer had lands to farm, faced a daunting future where they saw their identity denigrated and where they were a poor minority in their native land in a state where they were unwanted.

Evolving in these circumstances at the time Darwish started writing, and to a large extent until today, Palestinian literature written in Israel has been what Deleuze and Guattari called "a minor literature" (1986, 17). Deleuze and Guattari locate a minor literature in the repressed and censored dimensions of a culture. According to them, a minor literature evolves and is characterized by deterritorialization, political engagement, and collective articulation. In their discussion of Franz Kafka, they drew on the concept of a deterritorialized language as a vehicle for self-expression for the German-speaking Jews in pre-World War I Prague. The

Jews of Prague formed a minority that was "cut off from [the] masses" (Deleuze and Guattari 1986, 16) of Czech speakers around them and from the larger German-speaking world. The Palestinians were similarly cut off from the rest of the Arabic-speaking world, and their writings in Arabic were also cut off from the Jews of Israel, who were not interested in the least. Furthermore, the Hebrew language had made very few inroads to the Arab community before the establishment of Israel, and Palestinians who did write in Hebrew were practitioners of an even more minor literature.

The second feature of a minor literature, according to Deleuze and Guattari, appears as a strong political orientation in the works that comprise it. "Everything in them is political," whereby individual and psychological concerns of a minor literature articulate themselves in terms of "a political program" (17). "The cramped spaces of minor literature magnify each individual intrigue and connect it to politics" (17). The danger of a disappearing national and collective consciousness outside the nation urges the writer to forge alliances and participate in different configurations of identity, whereby the individual and the political/collective are in tandem.

A strong political orientation permeates the Darwish poems presented so far in this analysis. The poet was part of a generation that considered themselves a minority in the state of Israel, that was not intent on dismantling that state, and that wrote about the political dilemma in which they found their people embroiled. Even before Darwish came on the scene, several Palestinian intellectuals and artists had, in fact, forged alliances with Israeli political activists. Foremost among them is the novelist Emile Habibi, who joined the Israeli Communist Party MAKI (later renamed Rakah) in the late 1940s, bringing with him several other writers. MAKI, Rakah, and other Communist groups were primarily Jewish institutions and were thus allowed to print materials in Arabic. Through these Communist newspapers, Habibi and later Darwish—as well as other Arab authors—began to publish their work. Some Palestinian writers felt they had completely integrated their cause within a larger framework of the world's poor and dispossessed. The poet Tawfiq Ziyad, for example, positioned the Palestinian struggle from a global perspective and refused to devote his attention to fighting only Israeli injustice toward Palestinians. Instead, he urged Palestinian authors to engage in a global anticapitalist, anti-imperialist class struggle.

Closely linked to the political disposition of minor literature is a third feature—collective articulation. Deleuze and Guattari explain that the political element in minor literature assumes a kind of collective will operating within it, or the attempt to fashion such a will. "What each says individually already constitutes a common action," they contend (Deleuze and Guattari 1986, 17). Since the writing of minor literature originates in communities marked by a loss or the threat of erasure of national or collective identity, memories and other fragments of historical and cultural repositories need to be brought together. Here "literature finds itself positively charged with the role and function of collective, and even revolutionary, enunciation" (17). Darwish's poem "Identity Card" is a supreme example of a collective articulation. A dramatic monologue, it combines the biography of the poet's father with the poet's own anger to fashion a statement, which many Palestinians and Arabs elsewhere identified with.

Deleuze and Guattari's outline of the basic elements of a minor literature sounds a great deal like the stipulations for the production of a literature of commitment, which came to be called *adab al-iltizam* in Arabic. Influenced by social realism (and to some extent by Sartre's writings on engagement), the *adab al-iltizam* critics working in the 1950s, led by Salama Moussa in Egypt and Raif al-Khouri and Marun Abboud in Lebanon, emphasized mass communication as an essential property of committed literature, as well as the necessity of writing in the language of the people (Jayyusi 1977, 574). Men and women of letters were called upon to engage with the masses and to share in the sufferings and joys of the common people. Writers were also called upon to portray real life precisely, to explore the struggle between the classes, and to advocate heroism among the oppressed. Optimism and faith in the strength and determination of the masses should permeate literature; general and class understanding, rather than an individual point of view, should guide the literary work.

Darwish, in keeping with the poets of his generation, operated in an atmosphere where poetry, both recited and printed, had been established as a means of political action. Palestinian poets before Darwish were fully engaged in political agitation against the British—not just through their poetry but also through political organization and education. Among Palestine's early heroes was the poet 'Abdulraḥim Mahmoud, who was involved in militant activity against the British in the 1936 Palestinian Revolt and was forced to flee the country. In 1948, he returned to fight the Israeli army and died in battle. Thus the shaping of Darwish's poet persona had a preexisting model of the poet as political agent, a model that harkened back to the traditional Arab notion of the poet's role in the world, which survived quite intact into the modern era. Ancient classical Arab poet-warriors such as Imru-al-Qais, 'Antarah ibn Shaddad, Abi Firas al-Ḥamadani, and al-Mutannabi were either rulers or were seeking to become political leaders in their tribes or princedoms. Neoclassical poetry of the modern era also offered several examples of poets whose works reflected and influenced public opinion. The romantic mode that emerged in the Arab world in the twentieth century—as represented by Lebanese poet al-Akhtal al-Ṣaghīr (originally Bishara al-Khouri) and Tunisian poet Abulqasim al-Shabbi, among others—bore the strongest expression of Arab national longing for self-determination and independence from the colonizers.

Through these models of Arabic poetry written before 1948, Darwish was made conscious of poetry's history as a guiding discourse and tool for political change. Beginning with his first attempts at poetry, Darwish saw that both Palestinians and the Israeli authorities understood the power of poetry. Darwish first publicly appeared as a poet in grade school, where he recited a poem addressed to a Jewish youngster like himself who had the school supplies and educational possibilities he did not. News of the poem reached an Israeli military officer, and the young Darwish was accosted (Darwish 1971, 219–20). Darwish's five imprisonments over the course of his lifetime were sentences for poetic activity, such as traveling to recite his poems without being granted permission or for a poem published in a newspaper. His poetry therefore put him in direct confrontation with the Israeli authorities (al-Naqqāsh 1971, 110–13).

The Palestinians in Israel in the first decade after the Nakba understood and fostered the power of poetry to galvanize their community. Denied permission to organize to fight for their rights as citizens and residents of the state of Israel, and refusing to submit to government censorship for publication, Palestinian communities in the 1950s began to instead organize political rallies in which poetry featured prominently. During these rallies, the poets and political organizers involved were often harassed or arrested. Qahwajī (1972), Mustafa (1978), and Shihade (2011) report that thousands attended these gatherings where the poets persistently focused on themes of the land and village life, elucidating the concerns of Palestinian agricultural workers and farmers who had been deprived of their land, their social support networks, and their right to work independently and be taxed fairly. The fusion of poetry and political expression created in the minds of the Palestinians an association between the poetry they wrote and recited and the emergence of their political will to power. According to Qahwajī, poetry "encouraged the youth and those susceptible to being brought under the fold of Israeli hegemony, most likely in a subservient fashion, to seek a political and emotional discourse that uplifted them instead and herein lay the role of poetry in helping them counteract the Israeli government's effort to erase their Arab heritage through negligence" (1972, 284).

Darwish and other Palestinian poets began to appear during these festivities in the late 1950s and early 1960s. Their adoption of some of the more recent developments in Arabic poetry as they understood them (shorter lines, opposition to classical diction, and the use of everyday images and common objects as symbols), along with the influence of international revolutionary literature's emphasis on collective representation of the experiences of ordinary, working people, served the young poets in a politically expedient manner. These modern approaches brought the Palestinian poets closer to their people while elsewhere in the Arab world such poetic innovations and tamperings with treasured practices tended to alienate them. The largely semiliterate Palestinian population respected classical Arabic poetry, "but their poetry, the one in which they saw themselves most closely represented, was the vernacular form" (Kanafani 1966, 109). The modern poetic verse line, as presented by Darwish's generation, was shorter, lighter in diction, and played off a variety of metrical registers and rhyme schemes. It exhibited a proximity to the vernacular poetry and evoked a sense of exuberance and youthfulness rather than the somber authoritativeness of classical Arabic poetry. In essence "the poets of the resistance" writing inside Israel—as Darwish, Samih al-Qasim, Tawfiq Ziyad, and Sallim Jibran came to be known—kept up with the latest poetic developments in the other Arab capitals and, in doing so, managed to connect strongly with their fellow citizens. Rather than alienating a large chunk of their populace as other modernist poets such as Said 'Aql, Adonis (Ali Ahmad Said), and even committed poets like Şalah 'Abdul-Şabur and Khalil Ḥawi did, the young Palestinian poets in Israel succeeded in getting the populace to embrace the new poetry.

Another factor that should be noted is the extent to which Palestinian literature inside Israel, beginning with Darwish's generation, was, to some degree, a hybrid literature. A minor literature, as Deleuze and Guattari note, emerges partly out of isolation, and takes on particular inflections due to that isolation. The emergence of a new, rejuvenated Palestinian poetry inside the state of Israel, a poetry that had parted ways with earlier Palestinian poetry both formally and tonally, can be said to have begun in the early 1960s with the emergence of the first generation of bilingual Palestinian writers who spoke (and read) both Arabic and Hebrew. Political developments in the region and the emergence of a new generation of writers bent on playing an active role in their community's future clearly contributed to the birth of this new literature.

With modern Arab literature and Arabic translations of world literature generally unavailable, Hebrew became the second reading language of Darwish's generation, and for two decades it was their primary access to modern and ancient world literature (Wāzin 2006, 106). Darwish was influenced by Nazim Hikmet and Vladimir Mayakovski through Hebrew translation (Yahyá 2003, 182). He continued to read Lorca, whom he admired greatly, in Hebrew for the rest of his life.

Another undeniable influence on Darwish was the Hebrew Bible, which he drew on early in his career and continued to do so throughout his life, as is noted in later chapters (see Ibrahim 2005; Neuwirth 2008; and Shalat 1999). Darwish utilized biblical figures, such as Habakkuk, Isaiah, Elijah, and Jeremiah to voice the Palestinian cause. In a series of poems titled "Mazameer" (Psalms), written shortly after his departure from Israel, Darwish appeals to the Hebrew prophet Habakkuk, a minor early Jewish prophet who chronicled the Jews' suffering at the hands of their enemies. In response to Darwish's plaint on his people's suffering, Habakkuk says, "That is enough my son! / Your stories are in my heart. / Your stories are knives in my heart" (Darwish 2005, 2:133). Darwish's use of Habakkuk shows Darwish's strong familiarity with Jewish history and testifies to his knowledge of Hebrew literature, both ancient and modern, in which such allusions were common. Darwish and other Palestinian poets were "able to compare the Palestinians' experience with the Jewish diaspora, thus allowing them a way to demonstrate to the Israelis the truth about their suffering," writes Aḥmād al-Rifaʻi (1994, 132). The Hebrew psalms were particularly illuminating to Darwish both in poetic form and content, adding "a reverential element to his depiction of the Palestinian suffering" (1994, 43) and affirming the connections between both peoples' experiences.

As to the modern Israeli poets, Darwish stated that he competed with them so he could demonstrate his greater attachment and love for the land, and he continued to compete with them late into his career (Wāzin 2006, 123–24). Darwish admits to appreciating the Israeli poet Yehuda Amichai (1924–2000) and other Israeli poets he read while still in Israel (Shalat 1999, 153; Sulaiman 1984, 198). But it was Hayyim Bialik (1873–1934) who—among the Israeli poets— seems to have impressed Darwish most as he was starting out. Darwish first encountered Bialik when a Jewish high school teacher he adored instructed him "to read the Torah as a literary text, and to study Bialik regardless of his political enthusiasms, paying attention only to his poetic energy" (Darwish 1971, 222). Bialik's imagery in depicting the hardship of the Jewish Diaspora, which made him Israel's national poet, ran parallel to Darwish's own insistence on the end of Palestinian displacement and suffering under Zionist rule. Furthermore, al-Rifaʻi argues that Bialik's longing for a Zionist homeland, his sense of historical grievance, and his persistent calls for a committed literature to match the political ambitions of his people meet their match in Darwish's early work (1994, 63–107). Indeed, al-Rifa'i's comparative analysis of Darwish and Bialik's work is quite informative. Darwish manages, as al-Rifa'i illustrates, to sound out a vibrant and spontaneous body of poetry in his early work, while at the same time, effectively turning the Zionist emotive appeal inside out, arguing that it is the Palestinians who seek and deserve a peaceful existence on their homeland rather than their Zionist occupiers.

Darwish's familiarity with Hebrew, coupled with his desire to draw from and to speak outside the fold of traditional Arabic prosody, doubtlessly enriched his poetic project. We will address his engagement with and appropriation of Hebrew themes in greater depth when we turn to Darwish's post–Beirut period, especially the long poems in *Ara ma Urid (I See What I Wish to See)*, published in 1990. In the meantime, let us turn to analysis of Darwish's poems published during his first phase in Israel/Palestine to understand how he approached his role as a poet and as a cultural and political agent.

3

Poet under Occupation, 1964–1971

The underlying facts of Darwish's life as a young man, such as the marginalized and oppressed status of his community, the state of linguistic and cultural siege under which they lived, the intertwining of poetry and politics, and his familiarity with the literature of the colonizer, shaped him. Emerging in the early 1960s and starting from a lyrical standpoint of personal suffering, he set about to speak for his community as well as to reach out to his community's adversaries. I noted earlier how keen Darwish was to make a connection with his readers. The assumption of the burden of anger arising from a collective wound helps establish the poet as a spokesperson for his people. Darwish's voice was emboldened by his adherence to the basic contours and duties of *adab al-iltizam*, or committed literature, whereby the larger cause of the community supersedes the individual's suffering. His poems in this framework, as Darwish himself acknowledges in a poem titled "'An al-shi'r" ("On Poetry"), would be

> . . . colorless
> tasteless . . . voiceless
> unless they carry a lamp from house to house
> unless the simple folks understood their meaning.
> (Darwish 2005, 1:63; ellipses in original)

Poetry must move within the community like a light clarifying a political vision and must provide intellectual enlightenment. Ambitious as it may be, poetry has to be written in ways that simple folks can still understand. This combination of instruction, seriousness, and simplicity constitutes an aesthetic value within the *iltizam* framework that Darwish adopted. In Darwish's case, this general approach contained four aims that he went about fulfilling in his first decade of writing in Palestine. The first was to speak and foster a collective consciousness among the Palestinians in Israel and elsewhere; second, to help shape an empowered Palestinian subjectivity; third, to foster exuberance and enthusiasm as opposed to melancholy and, subsequently, subservience; and fourth, to demythologize the occupier and to communicate with him.

Speaking in WE

From its beginning, the state of Israel was not "willing to include Arab culture and the Arabic language as partners in the shaping of Israeli culture" (Ganim 2001, 162), even though a fifth of the state's citizens at the time of the Nakba were Arab. Kanafani (1966) and al-Naqqāsh (1971) report on the dearth of Palestinian Arabic-language work published in Israel in the 1950s and 1960s. As noted previously, al-Naqqāsh informs us that a total of sixty-four books were published in Arabic in Israel during the period from 1948 to 1967. Some of these books were published by Arabic-speaking Jews and expressed pro-Zionist attitudes and experiences. Most were romance narratives or *zajal* (amorous) poetry, deemed safe and apolitical by Israeli censors. The main venues for political/poetic expression were the aforementioned poetry festivals, which included poetic recitations but produced no publications. Kanafani adds that in Israel, many Palestinian funerals—not just the ones where the dead were victims of Israeli violence—became politicized. The funeral criers, reports Kanafani, wove resistance politics into their dirges (Kanafani 1966, 15–18). Subsequently, poets began to recite poetry at funerals that went beyond the elegiac occasion, poetry that expressed resistance to Israeli policies regarding the Palestinians inside the country. As such, written poetry was brought to a state of orality, and the poet had to become as much a performer as a writer. Darwish and his generation of poets came to a point where the privacy of poetic composition was quickly brought to the fore of public performance. He and the poets of his generation had no stage fright as they brought the audience with them to the page while writing their poems.

Let's turn to a poem from that period, "Wa 'ad fi kaffan" ("And He Returned . . . in a Shroud"), published in 1964, to see Darwish in action:

They say in our country,
  they say with sadness
about my friend who passed
  and returned in a shroud.

His name . . .
  Don't mention his name!
  Let's keep it in our hearts.
  Let's not let the word
  get lost in the air like ash.

Let him be a sensitive wound . . . no dressing
has found a way to it.
I fear, my loved ones, I fear O orphans,
I fear that we will forget him in the throng of names.
I fear he will melt in winter storms!
I fear that our wounds will fall asleep
inside our hearts.
I fear our wounds will sleep.
(Darwish 2005, 1:26–27)

The poem is an elegy for an innocent young man who left his
home and returned dead wrapped in a shroud. In the second
and third sections, which follow the aforementioned passage,
Darwish proves the young man's innocence through his lack
of experience in love and his lack of travel. In the fourth section, the poet turns to the young man's mother, addressing
her as "Mother," and advises her not to pull her "tears by the
root." He adds that she should leave in her "well of tears, two
tears / for tomorrow his father may die . . . or his brother / or
I, his friend" (30). It is only in the fifth and final section that
we learn the details of the young man's death:

They speak a great deal in our country
about my friend,
the fires of lead on his cheeks
his chest . . . his face.
Don't explain things!
I saw his wound,
I stared deep into his horizons . . .
My heart goes out to our children
and each mother that embraces a deathbed.
Friends of the faraway traveler,

* demonstrates

don't ask, "When will he return?"
Don't ask too much,
but ask: when
will our men wake up! (31)

As to be expected of an elegy with shades of melodrama, the poem is full of tears. The victim's innocence is emphasized to evoke sympathy, and his weeping mother is brought before us to be consoled. Yet despite this uninhibited sense of grief, and indeed the desire to evoke a sense of grief in the reader, the poet withholds some information. We learn only at the very end of the poem that the victim died violently, his corpse bearing "fires of lead on his cheeks / his chest . . . his face."

Keeping the victim's identity unknown will ensure his immortality, contends the poet. Darwish, except in a few elegies of his own friends, never mentions the names of "victims," especially in this early period when the emphasis is on raising collective consciousness. The presence of the victim's name will make him "disappear in a forest of names" (Darwish 2005, 1:26), but his essence can be preserved in a poem. The issue is not the victim's death, but the fear that the people's "wounds will die inside them" (27). The poet emphatically commands his listeners not to mention the victim's name, but to leave the victim nameless inside their hearts so their wounds remain alive. No one, therefore, should harbor a private grief for the victim; rather, the Palestinians as a collective should maintain an abstract and unified image of their victim as a symbol of their suffering and as an inspiration to bring the suffering to an end. The poet is the first to admit to this; he is speaking about his friend to all of his people—shaping his grief—and by sharing it, he is trying to conjure a form of empowerment. Indeed, even the deceased's mother is asked not to expend her sorrow.

The poet's job in this poem is to choreograph grief. The setting of the poem is theatrical; the poet is addressing a crowd. As he is about to mention the victim's name, and as he feels the crowd about to utter it, he boldly commands them not to do so. He establishes himself firmly as the primary mourner and informs us that the victim is his friend before we learn that the boy's mother is somewhere in the crowd. After he describes the victim's life, he turns to her and tells her before the listener/spectators how to manage her grief. As to the public's grief, the poet tells them how to act and gives his reasons. At the end of the poem, the poet again commands the people as to how they should address this tragedy. Do not ask about what will happen to the victim who lies still with his grieving mother beside him, he orders; rather, ask yourselves when will the men among you wake up.

That the poet turns his private grief into a call for collective action is to be expected in resistance literature. But I am still struck by the confidence of the poet's voice. He is secure in his knowledge of the victim; in fact, he knows things no one else can know: "I saw his wound / I stared deep into his horizons" (Darwish 2005, 1:27). No one else has had this vision, and it is this ability to see into others' horizons that emboldens the poet. He takes command of a public situation—indeed he turns the private into public—and the people are brought together in his grief. The experience enlightens them about their own situation and how they can gear up to change it.

Confident as the poet-speaker seems, however, he never uses the first-person-plural pronoun. Instead of starting off with "In our country we say," he somewhat abstracts the "we" into a "they," perhaps feeling the weight of spokesmanship. The poet-speaker projects no such shyness in the content of the poem, and we may understand his boldness in directing the traffic of emotion as a way to earn the use of the "we" and to speak for the community. Similarly, in the early poem "Hope," we see Darwish still resistant to speaking in "We," only addressing his community as "You." In fact, in his first seven books, Darwish has only three poems that use the first-person plural: "Ughniya" ("Song"), "'An al-ṣumud" ("Regarding Perseverance"), and "Nashīd" ("Anthem"). As Darwish evolves as a poet, his poems often use a thicket of pronouns, with multiple I's speaking to different you's, as well as different sets of we's speaking to plural you's. In this early stage, however, he achieves a sense of the collective mainly through the variety of voices he speaks with and the diversity of situations he engages in. As in "And He Returned . . . in a Shroud," we encounter a single voice that forcefully projects his predicament outwardly. The theatrical element and the presence of a responsive audience afford the speaker the chance to impact a large group of his aggrieved community and to ignite a simultaneous catharsis among them.

In utilizing his experience as a public poet performing his poetry, Darwish restages such encounters and mimetically recreates a moment of collective engagement and solidarity brought about by a simultaneous expression of grief. The poem and the dramatic situation structured within it enact and testify to "the confirmation of the solidity of a single community embracing characters, author and readers, moving onward through calendarical time" (Anderson

2006, 28). In this poem and elsewhere at this early stage in his career, Darwish writes to and of his community "as though their relationships with each other are not in the smallest degree problematic" (Anderson 2006, 28). As we saw in the poem discussed earlier, the poet presumes a collective consensus even as he works to create it. As such, the poet, speaking for and to his community through diverse speech acts and layered dramatic enactments, begins to play an important role in giving shape to individual sentiments and streaming them toward a collective consciousness and action.

Out of Victims and Martyrs

Shaping the Palestinian Subject

The poems discussed thus far demonstrate Darwish's efforts to perhaps build what Benedict Anderson (2006) called an "imagined community." Part of this process for Darwish involved shaping an imagined subjectivity as well. He calls upon the Palestinian community, "both as individuals and as collective," albeit in a masculine tone through the image of men awakening, "to invent itself" (Ḥussayn 1988, 130). Language and eloquence "together with the awakening of consciousness . . . become tools with which to shape a civilization and the individual" (130). Darwish's affirmative approach to literature falls into what advocates of *iltizam* literature have considered a necessity, mainly instilling heroism among the common people and inspiring optimism and faith in the oppressed people's just causes.

The difference, however, between the hope raised by revolutionary precepts and rhetoric and the reality of the situation at hand naturally points to the gap that literature has to bridge. We as readers often detect this gap within a text when the speaker in a poem begins with images of hardship and injustice and then moves toward a scene of hope and triumph for the underprivileged. Though placed mostly in reality, much of *iltizam* literature suffers from the frequency of what Aristotle called "improbable possibilities" in his *Poetics* (2007, 51). Stories fail to convince us, Aristotle argues, because the outcomes they propose—while they lie within the realm of the physically possible—are improbable given not only the world of the narrative itself but also the reality of the "real" world that the text is purportedly depicting.

One way to address this split between the need to depict a harsh reality and the equally important need to create literature that helps people imagine a way out of that reality is to write two sorts of texts, whether they be poems or stories, to serve these two different and often contradictory functions. The other possibility is to divide these functions according to genre. The latter seems to have been the bargain struck by Palestinian literature until well into the 1970s.

The two distinct voices of that era were Ghassan Kanafani (1936–1972) and Mahmoud Darwish. In Kanafani's hands, the novel and the short story focused on the harsh realities of Palestinian life. Kanafani's two novellas, *Rijal fil Shams* (*Men in the Sun*, 1963) and *'Aaid ila Haifa* (*Returning to Haifa*, 1970), are masterpieces in realism. The first centers on a group of Palestinian refugees on the Iraqi border who are trying to enter Kuwait illegally and who perish inside the tank of a water truck. The characters in this novel, who are victims of a war they did not provoke, experience occupation, displacement, and finally legal and political infringement against their pursuit of a decent livelihood.

Returning to Haifa recounts the experience of a slightly different kind of victimization—this time of a Palestinian couple who were forced out of Haifa in 1948 and who had accidentally left their infant at their soon-to-be-confiscated home. Returning to their native city of Haifa in 1967, after Israel occupied the West Bank, where they had settled in 1948, the couple visits their old apartment. There they find that their son has been adopted by a Jewish family and has grown to become a proud Israeli soldier.

Despite the fact that *Returning to Haifa* ends with an unconvincing glimmer of hope, both novels are realistic tragedies. They help deepen the reader's understanding of the Palestinians' anguish and trauma. And for the Palestinians themselves, or anyone identified with them, the novels are a great source of catharsis, encapsulating in their characters much of the Palestinians' painful history of military weakness, betrayal, and injustice, coupled with unmitigated misfortune.

In his poetry and in interviews addressing the early stages of his career, Darwish attests to Kanafani's definition of a social and political orientation to literature, which Kanafani practiced and theorized. Wielding poetry as a mass-communication tool for political advocacy, Darwish attempts to address the travails of the individual Palestinian and offers appropriate metaphors and personae to serve as symbolic representations of transformation and empowerment.

Herein, I believe, lies the role that poetry, as opposed to realist fiction, played as a political, cultural discourse for the Palestinians living in and outside of Israel: poetry attempted to create an image of the Palestinian as larger than life, a noble figure who suffers unbearable misfortunes but who holds to life-affirming ideals. Poetry's function was nothing short of "the restoration of individual subjectivity" (Abū Shāwir 2003, 176). Focusing on providing the appropriate symbols and metaphors, Darwish's poetry and that of his peers, according to Abū Shāwir, was bent on "exploring the capacity for metamorphosis" (2003, 177). Life-affirming metaphors, he adds, have "a capacity to endlessly recycle their meaning and produce unpredictable proliferations" (177) in the concrete lives of individuals.

Capturing this sense of lopsided fate that Palestinians faced, Darwish offers in a poem titled "About a Human Being" the hard facts of Palestinian existence and attempts to burst them:

They placed chains on his mouth,
tied his hands to the stones of the dead
and said, you are a murderer.

They took his food and drink, they took his field
and threw him in the prison cell of the dead
and said you are a thief.

They expelled him from all harbors,
took his young beloved
and said, you are a refugee.

You, whose eyes and hands are bloodied,
night will dissolve;
the detention cell will not live forever
nor the chains.

Nero died, but Rome did not die—
she fights with her eyes—
and grains in a wheat plant die
only to fill the valley with new shoots.
(Darwish 2005, 1:20–21)

Darwish here begins by abstracting the Palestinian subject, writing about a nameless victim, providing a real situation that is on the cusp of becoming myth. Such distance between the Palestinian reader and this portrait of him only deepens the sense of tragedy, as this representation offers many of the basic facts of the Palestinian experience whereby the victim of Nazism becomes the Israeli offender, the dispossessed Palestinian becomes a thief, and the one rooted to the place becomes a refugee.

Setting this drama in motion, Darwish then turns the poem around and addresses the reader, who has become identified with the victim. The poet-speaker assures him, basing his argument on history and the laws of nature, that his tragedy will end because it is an abomination to both human history and nature. Human history does not allow for such injustice to continue in perpetuity, and nature has the mechanisms to eventually undo it. The brief reversal of the human and the natural order will be corrected.

In his predicament, the Palestinian does not lie still, but rather strongly expresses his defiance and indeed his indestructibility. Darwish provides several representations of the former—foremost among them the image of the Palestinian, or the Palestinian poet-speaker, as someone who is being crucified. Images of crucifixion permeate Darwish's poetry at this time, with the cross as a site of defiance:

They raised a cross against the wall.
The whiplash on my skin was a fan.
And the stomping of their feet
was a song saluting me: O master!
(Darwish 2005, 1:111)

We note here too Darwish's strategy of direct reversal. The whip's lash becomes soothing like a fan. The beatings the speaker receives from the soldiers become an acknowledgment of his superiority.

In another poem, the poet tells his listener, "We will make of our gallows and crosses, ladders to the promised day [of deliverance]" (Darwish 2005, 1:158). The image of the cross becomes a force for growth and resurrection in a more elaborate fashion in the passage that follows:

The singer on the cross of pain,
his wound glowing like a star,
expressed everything to the people
around him, everything except regret:
"This way I have died as I stand
and standing I die like a tree.
This way my cross becomes
a platform or a maestro's baton.
This way the nails of this cross
become musical strings.
This is how rain falls,
this is how trees grow." (96–97)

The multiple reversals offered here open up to a cosmic, utopian vision. Personal pain in the singer's wound becomes a star, a light that illuminates others. The cross, turned into a tree standing tall, becomes a symbol of glory and durability rather than death and punishment. The crucified singer sees in the wood and nails of the cross a whole orchestra on stage—thus creating a multiplication of him and an expansion of his single voice into a larger musical performance. Then the music itself becomes a catalyst for life as it returns to and entices the forces of nature toward nurturing and growth. Once the music begins to play, we discover that in the singer's crucifixion lies the secret of life's rejuvenation.

The symbol of the cross takes on a slightly more convoluted manifestation as the speaker addresses his beloved in this passage from "To a Lost One":

If it fell into my eyes,
that cloud of tears
that circled your black eyes,
I will then bear all the earth's sadness
as a cross
on which martyrs grow
as the earth grows small
and as your tear drops water
the sands in children's poems.
(Darwish 2005, 1:239)

Darwish again is creating a mystical relationship between human effort and the natural elements. As in the relationship between music and vegetative growth in the previous passage, here the poet establishes a similar relationship between the cosmic and the human. The poet's sadness becomes a cross on which human martyrs grow as the earth becomes smaller. The beloved's tears penetrate the world of the real and enter the world of imagination to irrigate the arid sands in children's poems, fostering growth in their imaginations and their inner nature. Death begets life, the human penetrates the material, and the tangible penetrates the spiritual. In offering this imaginative expansion of the Palestinian psyche, Darwish repeatedly stresses the generative and transformative potential of the Palestinians' struggle for justice.

Lover of the Feminized Nation

In his effort to foster solidarity among the Palestinian collective and to redeem Palestinian suffering, Darwish's first four volumes largely focus on public concerns that all citizens share. The impact of colonial oppression covers all spheres, and the struggle over land, racial equality, national self-determination, and social injustice penetrates all aspects of life to the point that "it is difficult to separate what is public and associated with the national and what is private and associated with the individual in his daily life" (Abūbakr 1997, 69). Obstacles of mobility, economic repression, and the threat of detention begin to impact the shape and nature of intimate relations. Romantic relationships become one of the fronts on which the poet fights for his and his people's freedom.

Darwish's early poems begin by using love as a motif to assert the Palestinians' common humanity and evolve to portray the various manifestations of Palestinian suffering.

What would provoke people if we walked in the light of
    day
and I carried your handbag for you, and your umbrella

and took your lips by a corner wall
and stole a kiss?
(Darwish 2005, 1:78–79)

Politics hardly appear in this poem. The amorous young poet wonders what harm his expression of affection would cause, and wonders why people would be upset by it. The sentiments expressed here are perhaps more daring than those expressed in earlier Arabic romantic poems, which would have fogged up even this tame love. Darwish's beloved is real, not imagined; she carries a handbag and an umbrella. Still, the poem, like its romantic predecessors, is simply seeking personal freedom and the right to feel and express affection. Later in the poem, we read, "From the well of my tragedy, I call out to your eyes / to carry the liquor of light to my veins" (79). We can perhaps insert the Palestinian predicament as his tragedy, but nothing in the poem itself suggests that. The poet-speaker here is simply lamenting his inability to express his love.

The poet's political activism—his engagement and struggle—become more apparent later as the cause of his separation from his beloved:

I have distributed my flowers
among the dispossessed, my flowers,
and wrestled with the wolves.
Then I returned to my place
where the ring of her laughter does not greet me
nor the caress of her kiss
the flutter of her whisper . . .
Friends, take the lamp, the poems, the solitude,

take these cigarettes, these newspapers
blackened like night
for I have returned to my place
and I feel destitute in my home.
I have lost all my flowers
and the secret of the source,
that one light
in the depth of my tragedy . . . (39–40)

In this setting of metaphorical wilderness, the poet shares flowers with his dispossessed loved ones and wrestles with wolves that endanger his and his people's survival. Whether it amounts to all he can do for them or it supplements his wrestling with the wolves, beauty is at the center of the struggle and his communion with his people. His work forces him to live away from his beloved, and he is ready to give everything to be with her, offering his poems and his writings to his friends and to his kin. The beloved is therefore the source of his inspiration, even "the secret of the source," and her presence in his life has kept him at his work of expounding hope and wrestling with the occupiers, but now he is distraught.

Darwish further develops the subject of love as an arena of struggle for the shaping of Palestinian subjectivity in the midst of oppression. He does this by adopting the very role of 'Ashiq min Filasṭin (*Lover from Palestine*) as his most consistent persona in his first decade of writing. He offers a portrait of the Palestinian—dedicated to his homeland, society, noble human values, and his beloved—as a human ideal, not simply a person with a just cause. Darwish's major transformation of the traditional love motif is the conflation of the beloved with the nation. He is the denied lover in the following passage:

Your lips are honey, and your hand
a cup of wine
for others . . .
And the silk of your breast, your basil, your dew
are a comfortable bed
for others.

And I am the sleepless one lying by your black walls;
I am the sand's thirst, the shiver of nerves in firesides.
Who can shut the door before me?
What tyrant, what fiend?
I will love your nectar
even though it is poured in the cups of others . . . (18–19)

Precise tactile imagery complicates matters for the Israeli censor here. The poem is sensual and evocative, capturing the poet-speaker's loyalty to his beloved and his outrage at his circumstances. Unpacking the symbols of the poem readily renders a political reading. The lover's loyalty persists despite the beloved's preoccupation; we do not see her willingly offer her lips or her body as a cup or bed for others, but she nonetheless belongs to the others. The poet adds that the beloved is forced into this situation by a tyrant or a fiend. The lover cannot reach his beloved's nectar, but he shall not be moved. Insisting instead to remain by her walls, blackened perhaps by war or by forced entry, he lies waiting. He cannot be barred from her since he is the elements themselves, the sand's thirst and the sparks in the household fire.

The eroticization of the homeland becomes more explicit in later poems in this period. "Reading My Beloved's Face" begins with a supposed real or human beloved in whose eyes the poet begins to see manifestations of what could be the Palestinian trauma and the potential for continued existence and renewal:

> When I gaze at you
> I see lost cities
> and a crimson time.
> I see the reason for death and pride.
> I see a new language yet to be recorded
> and gods passing on foot
> before an astounding surprise.
>
> . . . and you spread before me
> lines of creatures that cannot be named.
> My country is nothing but these eyes
> that turn the land into a body. (310)

Looking into his beloved's eyes, the poet sees his nation's history of lost cities and decades of bloodshed. He also sees the reasons to fight for the nation and the awe it will project, forcing gods to walk barefoot before her, astounded by her beauty. The end of the passage further complicates the conflation between the beloved and the nation, making it impossible to discern where the beloved's body begins and the land ends. The poet by now cannot see his country in any other way. The country is shaped by his (or the beloved's) eyes, which refuse but to give the land a desired human shape.

The eroticization, or more precisely, the feminization of the land, opens up new horizons for speaking of the nation. It is a clear departure from traditional approaches to the call for struggle in Palestinian poetry written before Darwish. His voice is personal and allows for a specific persona to emerge whose presence is marked by new imagery. A crimson time, gods passing on foot, basil, dew in the sand's thirst, and the shiver of nerves in firesides—these phrases were new to Arabic poetry and are generally secular, bearing no Islamic or traditional Arab echoes. The establishment of this specific relationship between Palestinians and Palestine bears the seeds of a rejuvenated nationalism that arises from new, native symbols as opposed to the symbols of Palestine within the broader Pan-Arab nationalism, which were largely reliant on religious associations. In poems written after the 1967 war, in which the West Bank and Gaza were occupied by Israel, Darwish begins to speak explicitly about breaking away from Arab *wissaya* or tutelage. In this tactile imagery of Palestine and in his erotic rendition of the country, Darwish, in effect, undertakes this objection to Pan-Arab guardianship long before he voices it. Writing from within Palestine, his poem does not express "a feeling of longing for something absent, but a feeling of brute dispossession" (Sulaiman 1984, 198). The land is akin to the beloved: visible and inaccessible.

And though he worked within the Israeli Communist Party, Darwish refused to address the Palestinian problem as only one among the just causes of the oppressed. He was determined to devote his energy to it alone. Here he addresses his fellow Palestinian Communists:

> Do not tell me
>> I wish I were a bread baker in Algeria
>> to sing with a fellow revolutionary . . .
> Do not tell me
>> I wish I were a waiter in a café in Havana
>> to sing of the victories of the downtrodden . . .

My friend,
  The Nile will never pour into the Volga
  or the Congo, or the Jordan into the Euphrates.
  Each river has a source, a stream, a life.
  My friend, our land is not barren.
  Each land will have its birth.
  Each dawn will have a rendezvous with a rebel.
  (Darwish 2005, 1:53)

Darwish's poetry begins to facilitate Palestinian ownership of the cause by establishing a relationship with the land that arises from their experiences on it. The land is female; it is fertile and will give birth to its dawn from and with its local elements. The eroticization of the land provides a metaphor for belonging that approximates the intimacy, passion, and emotional turmoil of romantic relationships. Erotic love as a metaphor for attachment to the homeland helps the individual and the collective weather the various difficulties they are bound to encounter in a long, everlasting relationship.

Finally, Darwish's employment of the love motif as a way of speaking and belonging to the land provides a response to Israeli writing and the claims it makes for historical Palestine. Darwish had declared openly that he was in competition with the Israeli poet Yehuda Amichai to prove that he loved the land more. Darwish understood that he who can "describe the land better can thus lay a stronger claim to it" (Sulaiman 1984, 199). Poetry becomes an act of naming, and eroticizing the land fits Darwish's understanding of the Palestinians' relationship with it. Comparing his and other Palestinians' relationship to the land, Darwish states: "We excavated this land neither in mythical dreams nor in the illustrated pages of an old book, nor did we create it in the way companies and institutions are established. It is our father and mother. We did not, either, buy it through an agency or a shop, and no one had to convince us to love it. We identify ourselves as its pulse and marrow of its bone. It is therefore ours, and we belong to it" (1971, 8–9). Darwish here offers a kind of checklist, and all the elements he cancels out lead him toward an understanding of the land as a living being. Palestinians did not discover Palestine through myth or through academic or literary pursuits; their attachment to the land is not religious or ideological. Their relationship does not proceed through commerce or politics. The land is like a body; it has a pulse, marrow, and bone; the land is the Palestinians' procreative lineage ("our father and mother") and their future.

Demythologizing (and Humanizing) the Adversary

Darwish's utilization of the erotic motif to describe his attachment to the land aims to affirm the legitimacy of his belonging to the place of his birth. His erotic nationalism offers a secular and humanistic form of belonging to counter the religious and racially exclusive form of belonging that Zionism offers. Whether inside or outside Israel, Palestinians on the left, like Darwish, felt compelled to demonstrate their faith in an inclusive society and to provide a vision of it for their Israeli adversaries as an alternative to a perpetual state of conflict. For many Palestinians, their distrust of the Israelis contended with their despair at their ability to ever achieve a fair political solution to their suffering. This was especially true after the 1967 war, in which their neighboring Arab armies suffered humiliating defeats, and after which more Palestinian territory fell to Israeli occupation. Darwish felt the need to explore the life experiences of his adversaries for their sake and for his people's sake to find the humanity of the other and, by doing so, to bolster his own subjectivity. Darwish's effort in this area did not begin with poetry. In numerous essays and articles that appeared in Arabic publications of the Israeli Communist Party (Rakah), Darwish expended serious effort to engage Israeli intellectuals and the Israeli public at large in dialogue regarding the oppressive conditions that Palestinians in Israel faced. He attempted to expose Israeli writers to Palestinians "who believe in the possibility of the two peoples living together in peace and in cooperation" on the same land, "provided that both populations are granted the same, and equal, rights" (Darwish 1971, 58). In addition to Darwish, who was jailed several times and placed under house arrest for a long stretch, other Palestinian writers faced similar treatment. During the 1950s, novelist and newspaper editor "Emile Habibi, among others" was "frequently arrested for periods of nine months and more" (Pappe 2011, 83). Pappe reports that during the 1960s,

> The best-known Palestinian poets in Israel in that period were either under house arrest or in jail for their more nationalist poems (although all of them had a sizeable share of love poems and more general poetry). When Samih al-Qasem published his collection *Wa yakunu 'an y'ati ta'ir al-ra'd (And the Thunderbird Will Arrive)* in March 1969, all copies were confiscated and the poet was arrested for not submitting parts of the book to the censor before publication. Two months later, the writers and journalists Salem Jubran and Ahmad Khaṭib were put under house arrest for publishing nationalist poetry. (Pappe 2011, 125)

That same year, 1969, Darwish was himself kept under house arrest, a ruling that was repeatedly renewed by the courts. Darwish had helped arrange meetings of Palestinian (Arabic) and Israeli (Hebrew) writers, and in several essays published at the time documented the areas of agreement and the obstacles that Israeli writers faced in supporting Palestinian writers—who are also Israeli citizens—persecuted by the Israeli government. Darwish responded positively to such interactions and saw in them "important turning points in changing the Israelis' attitude toward dialogue with Arabs" (Darwish 1971, 72). At one point, Darwish distributed a survey among Israeli writers asking them the following questions: "If you were an Arab (Palestinian) writer, if you were in my place, if your people faced the same issues, what would you do? Would you behave the way I do?" (1971, 88). Darwish collected some of these answers and published them in the newspaper *Al-Ittiḥad*. His editorials in the same newspaper also provided concise and interesting responses to Israeli attitudes toward Palestinians. In these articles, Darwish quotes Israeli government officials at length, as well as from official documents. Darwish also provides summaries and analyses of Israeli literary and cultural studies. Collected in his *Shai' 'an al-Waṭan* (*Something about the Homeland*), these articles are adept at constructing a dialogue that had not quite taken shape.

Darwish's poetry discussed thus far provides ample depictions of the Palestinians' suffering, their dedication to the land, and their aspirations toward self-determination. Though dedicated to instill a spirit of resistance, pride, and self-reliance among the Palestinians, Darwish nonetheless consistently called for peaceful coexistence between

Palestinians and Israelis. As a member of Rakah, he faithfully toed the party line, promoting peaceful coexistence between Israelis and Palestinians within the borders of Israel. Darwish did, however, verbally support the armed resistance to Israeli occupation of the West Bank and Gaza (1971, 76). Within Israel's 1948 borders, he called for political action and worked to penetrate Israeli intellectual circles. Darwish was aware that "the Zionist system feared more than anything else to be impressed, or to intermingle, with the culture of the Arabs in the same area" (Shalat 1999, 145). He gave numerous interviews with Israeli newspapers and magazines, regularly wrote editorials in the form of open letters to Israeli officials, and was keen on being translated into Hebrew (148).

Most interesting in this context are the poems Darwish wrote in Israel before 1970, in which he actively attempts to understand Israelis. These poems provide compelling portraits of Israeli characters and demonstrate exceptional empathy on his part. Giving the majority of their lines to the Israeli speakers, these poems engage Israeli characters in intimate dialogue, teasing out their vulnerabilities, aspirations, and contradictions. By displaying his capacity for empathy, Darwish "was trying to find ways of igniting similar empathy among the Israelis" (Baydūn 1999, 250).

One of Darwish's best-known poems of that period was devoted to Rita, a young Israeli woman. Rita emerged as a character in Darwish's early volumes of poetry and continued to appear late into his career. Darwish begins the interaction with Rita as a story of prohibited love, made impossible by Israel's militancy. "Between Rita and my eyes, a rifle," writes Darwish of his beloved, who is a conscript in the Israeli army (2005, 1:200). Darwish's poet-speaker is devoted to Rita, whom he had known since they were young. "I remember how she clung to me, / how on my arm a sweet braid fell" (200). They were lovers for two years "before this rifle came along" (201). The poem depicts the possibility for instinctive, affectionate human connection—the poet-speaker found Rita beautiful, and she found him kind and trusted him. Dedicated to their love for each other, they "made vows on the sweetest of drinks"; thus bonded, they were "reborn." Then suddenly "the city / swept away all its serenades / and swept my Rita too" (202). The speaker is aware that he may have been deceiving himself in thinking that the world, represented by the city, would let him continue this relationship with Rita. He had been dreaming, perhaps, when reality interrupted their affair. "Deep into morning / fell my moon" (202), he says, suggesting that the light he offered could not withstand the harsh reality represented by morning light. Rita simply leaves him and is swept away with the force of society's intervention. What separates them is the rifle given to Rita that forces her to turn her "honey-colored eyes" away from him.

The poem "A Soldier Dreams of White Lilies" offers an example of friendship between an Israeli soldier and a Palestinian named Mahmoud, a stand-in for the poet. Mahmoud narrates the poem, and begins with this description of the Israeli soldier:

> He dreams of white lilies,
> an olive branch
> and of her breast in evening bloom.
> He dreams, he told me, of a bird,
> a lemon blossom,

and he did not philosophize his dream.
He did not understand things
except in the way he felt them, smelled them.
He understood, he told me, that "the country"
is to drink my mother's coffee
to return home safely in the evening. (2005, 1:203)

The symbol of an olive branch expressing the Israeli soldier's desire for peace does not escape our attention, being introduced so early in the poem. The white lilies are a new symbol in Darwish's poems at this point, perhaps emphasizing the soldier's attraction to nonnative flowers. But the lemon blossom is native and is one of Darwish's repeated images, as well as the birds' singing. Darwish makes the soldier resemble himself even further by describing his longing for his mother's coffee. This image comes right out of one of Darwish's best-known poems, "To My Mother," which had become an informal Palestinian anthem after its publication in *'Ashiq min Filasṭin* (*Lover from Palestine*, 1966). In that poem Darwish writes, "I long for my mother's bread / and my mother's coffee / and my mother's touch . . ." (106). The Israeli soldier expresses the same longings as the poet himself. Providing further positive images of the soldier, the poet-speaker informs us that the soldier's mother, like the grieving mothers who fill Darwish's poems of this period, also "wept silently when they took [the soldier] / to a position on the front" (205).

Darwish's stand-in in this poem attempts to project objectivity by repeating the phrase "he told me." The use of this journalistic trope distances the two characters and lessens the identification between them. It is as if Darwish is telling his Palestinian, Arab, and Israeli audiences that he, the poet, did not make up this portrait, that he is merely reporting what the soldier told him. The soldier speaks half the lines in the poem (59 out of 118). The poet-speaker of this poem poses only a few questions, and they take up about a tenth of the poem itself. When the poet speaks about the soldier, he mostly describes his physical actions: "He adjusted his posture, / toyed with the folded newspaper," "He told me about his first love," and so on:

> He told me about his departure,
> how his mother
> wept silently when they took him
> to a position on the front.
> And his mother's burning voice
> turned a new wish under his skin:
> If only doves would grow in the ministry of defense,
> if only doves would grow . . .
>
> He smoked, and told me
> as if fleeing a blood swamp:
> I dreamt of white lilies,
> an olive branch,
> a bird embracing the morning
> on a lemon bough.
> —"What did you see?"
> —"I saw what a red boxthorn can do.
> I planted it in the sand, in chests, in bellies."
> —"And how many did you kill?"
> —"It's hard to count them . . .
> but I won a medal."

I asked him, hurting myself as I did.
—"Describe one victim to me, if you can."
He adjusted his posture,
toyed with the folded newspaper
and said to me as if singing a song:
—"Like a tent, he fell on the gravel
and embraced the shattered planets.
There was a crown of blood on his wide brow,
his chest without medals,
because he was not good at killing,
maybe a farmer, a laborer, or a traveling salesman.
Like a tent he fell on the gravel, and died.
His arms
stretched like two dry streams
and when I searched his pockets
for his name, I found two pictures,
one of his wife,
one of his little girl . . ."
—"Were you sad," I asked.
He answered, interrupting me,
—"Mahmoud, my friend,
sadness is a white bird
that never comes near battlefields,
and soldiers commit a grave sin
when they fall sad. I was a machine there,
blowing rose-colored fire
that turned space into a black bird."

He told me about his first love,
and later
about distant cities
and the reaction to the war . . . (205–8)

Darwish's poet-speaker distributes information quite deliberately. The soldier's positive aspects depicted in the departure scene as his mother wept, his affection for his beloved, and "the new wish under his skin" for doves to "grow in the ministry of defense" (204), are all stated by the poet-speaker in third person. It is the soldier himself, speaking in first person, who reveals himself to us as a killing machine, a fire-blowing monster.

The renowned Palestinian critic Yūsuf al-Khaṭīb objected to Darwish's sympathetic portrait of the Israeli soldier, refusing "to go along with Darwish's experiment" (al-Khaṭīb 1968, 90). Al-Khaṭīb, who was responding to al-Naqqāsh's admiration of Darwish's work here, adds that the Israeli soldier is no different from any of Hitler's officers "who fulfill his military obligations in battle, then returns to drink and weep while gazing at a photo of his wife and infant child" (91). Al-Naqqāsh, responding to al-Khaṭīb, states that Darwish's portrait of the soldier "reveals, alongside the humane aspect in this Jewish soldier, the degree to which this simple human being had been mangled and turned into a mass murderer" (al-Naqqāsh 1971, 273). Darwish's use of inserted monologue in this poem further suggests that the soldier is fully aware of his crimes and that he is trapped in this vicious role, unable or perhaps unwilling to be anything else.

This suggests to me that the poem succeeds in demonstrating the Israeli soldier's ordinary humanity, his familial bonds, his desire for peace and love, and his overall simplicity. But something at the political level—the heroism of the radio and newspaper, the fiery speech and lecture—have made his "way of love" a rifle. Darwish's Israeli soldier is both a pitiable figure and a sociopath. Presenting him to his Palestinian readers, Darwish demythologizes the Israeli soldier by painting him as a victim of ideology who prefers his simple desires. For Israeli readers, Darwish demonstrates through this dramatization that he does not object to this soldier's Jewishness or national background, only his present politics and ideology.

Darwish, however, does interrogate his soldier about issues of legitimacy and belonging to the land, even as he expresses sympathy. As mentioned earlier, the soldier is dreaming of white lilies on the arid hills and plains of Palestine. When the soldier says "'my country / is to drink my mother's coffee,'" the poet-speaker states, "I asked: 'and the land?'" (Darwish 2005, 1:203). Promptly the soldier answers, "I don't know it" (203). The soldier goes on to explain that his belonging is shallow and imposed upon him. "'They taught me to love her love, / and I never felt my heart its heart'" (204). "Would you die for it?" the speaker asks him, and again the soldier answers curtly, "'No!'" (204). He is willing to kill for the nation, but not to die for the land. The poet, upholding Darwish's standard of love for the land as the equivalent of romantic love, insists on the nature of this relationship with the land, and reveals the soldier's lack of affection for it:

And how was its love?
Did it sting like the sun, like longing?
He answered me, confronting:
—"My way of love is a rifle
and a festival retrieved from old ruins,
the silence of an old statue
lost in time, of an unknown source." (204–5)

Darwish lyrically expresses here what he had said elsewhere, regarding the Israelis' sense of belonging to the land, and how it arises from mythical dreams and illustrated pages of old books, not from ages of physical contact and historical corporeal familiarity. The soldier, standing in for other Israelis, belongs to the land by excavating nonliving, human-made things—ruins and statues—while the Palestinian's love for the land stings as if it is a living creature. Darwish also suggests that all the victories for which the Israeli soldier has won medals, and for which he cares more than those whom he killed, do nothing to create a sense of belonging.

To highlight the difference between the Palestinian sense of belonging to the land and that of the Israelis who have fought for it and won, Darwish's speaker, even after hearing of the soldier's travails and heavy heart, expresses surprise at the soldier's desire to leave "the homeland." The poet seems to suggest that the Palestinian simply cannot fathom the idea of leaving his homeland, no matter the burden that being there exerts upon him. The irony of course is obvious—those who are being killed and oppressed cannot fathom leaving the land, while those doing the conquering are so half-hearted about their belonging that they are ready to leave. This difference for Darwish's Palestinian readers, this unshakable attachment to the land, marks their eternal advantage over the Israelis, who resemble the lilies they dream of on the land to which they are not native.

4

Poet of National Liberation, 1971–1986

Referring to "A Soldier Dreams of White Lilies" in a 1969 interview with an Israeli magazine, Darwish says "I wish to express pride in my own humanity in that I am the first Arab poet to portray an Israeli soldier, even after the June '67 War, in his full human essence." (Darwish 1971, 231). He goes on to inform his Israeli readers about how the poetry of his generation of Palestinians living in Israel had gained a great deal of attention in the Arab world, with critics and readers well aware that "the starting point for these poets is the recognition of the rights of Jews and Arabs to exist in Palestine" (334). The pairing of a clear political stance with an aesthetic achievement that facilitates the breakdown of psychological barriers exemplifies Darwish's sense of how poetry and politics ought to progress in step together. The poets of his generation are working on both sides of the conflict, he explains, decreasing animosity toward Israelis among Arabs and demonstrating to Israelis a capacity for understanding. In Darwish's view, the poet's art and his presence in society can help others make the imaginative leap toward action in a time of crisis.

In interviews and articles on the dialogues he and other Palestinian writers had with their Israeli counterparts in the late 1960s, Darwish seemed confident that the Palestinian side was ready for such a leap and that poetry had helped galvanize them to act in a unified manner. For those inside the state of Israel, the struggle for equality as citizens was to be conducted through "peaceful protest and opposition" (Darwish 1971, 234). He supported the Palestinians' armed struggle to end Israeli occupation and to establish their own state in the West Bank and Gaza. Furthermore, he argued that the Palestinians inside and outside the state of Israel were capable of speaking for themselves and needed no Arab tutelage. Dialogue between Palestinians and Israelis, he felt, would assist both sides in establishing some sort of trust, but real exposure to the Palestinians would be best found in their poetry "where national belonging is woven with our universal and human belonging" (236).

Examining the context of Darwish's poetry and the statements he makes in interviews, it is fair to wonder about the reach of Darwish's message. When a poet addresses a political issue in a poem, we assume that he has someone in mind. In the case of the Arab world, people were indeed listening to Palestine's poets. As soon as the pan-Arab literary scene discovered Darwish and the other Palestinian poets inside Israel, legions of poets and critics began to heap praise upon them and even to hang the Arab world's hopes on them. One of the Arab world's most popular and esteemed poets at the time, Nizar Qabbani, who had been a model for Darwish, placed Darwish's generation of Palestinian poets at the forefront and handed them the reins to Arab poetry.

In a chapbook of poems titled *Shu'arā' al-arḍ al-muḥtal-lah* (*Poets of the Occupied Land*) Qabbani declares poetry dead in the Arab world (Qabbani 1968, 10) after the *naksa* (defeat) of the 1967 Six-Day War. The poets of his day speak with "castrated" lips and use castrated words (13). They have become the rulers' mule drivers (*hudhi*) (13) who brandish their whips to keep the Arab people marching on the course drawn for them. In that atmosphere of oppression and despair, the poets of Palestine, such as Darwish, Tawfiq Ziyad, and Fadwa Tuqan, present a breath of fresh air and a chance of salvation for Arab poetry and the Arab body politic at large. The poets of the Arab world can learn from Darwish and his fellow Palestinian poets "how the drowned can sing in their well. / We learn from you what poetry can become," (12) declares Qabbani. Darwish did not react to these lines by Qabbani, whom he admired greatly. But he did respond to similar burdensome urging and unqualified praise by calling on Arab critics to cease pouring their "ruthless love" (Darwish 1971, 25) upon him and his fellow young poets.

On the other side, as Darwish had noted, the Israelis, writers, and the public were not keen on listening to the Palestinian poets who were fellow citizens of their country. Despite several attempts at dialogue, the Palestinian and Israeli writers remained divided as to what the central issues ought to be. For the Palestinian writers, the cause of the tension between them and the state of Israel was the "result of land confiscation, discrimination, exclusion, lower education, higher unemployment and lower income" (Schultz 2003, 74). Palestinian activism in Israeli politics, which Darwish had been active in through Rakah, was an example of what Smooha (1989) called the "Israelization" and "Palestinification" taking place simultaneously among Palestinians living in Israel. Palestinian integration within Israeli society had begun as soon as the Israeli government allowed it, opening sector by sector, and could be seen in their "participation in institutions of higher education, mobilization for Knesset participation and their rights, in popular culture, in the labor market, etc." (Schultz 2003, 78).

Very little of this seemed to matter to the Israeli writers Darwish tried to engage in the 1960s. For the vast majority of them, the cause of the Palestinians' sufferings was their hatred of Israel. The hardships the Palestinians faced and their nonintegration were unfortunate results of protective measures established by the Israelis due to wariness of the Palestinians' loyalty (Darwish 1971, 68). Some of the Israeli writers were indignant at the Palestinians. Dahlia Ravikovich, one of Israel's leading poets, left a meeting with Palestinian authors saying, "I came to this meeting a socialist and I leave a fascist," blaming the Palestinians for turning her into one (Darwish 1971, 79). Most indicative of the Israeli writers' refusal to acknowledge their Palestinian counterparts is what Darwish perceived as a double standard. He noted how Israeli intellectual circles regularly responded to the imprisonment, harassment, and censorship of writers in all parts of the world, but remained silent as these actions were taken by the Israeli authorities against Palestinians (50).

Darwish's fifth and last imprisonment in Israel created a qualitatively different threat to his sense of agency. In his four previous imprisonments, the charges were for traveling without permission (1965), political incitement (1965, 1966), and eluding detention during a state of emergency (1967). His last imprisonment, in 1969, took place after Palestinian militants blew up several houses in Haifa. The Israeli authorities detained him in the case, thus connecting him with military activities against the state. This association with militancy would have set Darwish on a different course of interaction with the Israeli legal system. Had he been deemed a terrorist he would have been charged under a different set of laws, and his temporary detention orders would have been renewed endlessly.

In a statement he released a year after leaving Israel for Moscow, Darwish writes: "I had become filled with a feeling that I was no longer able to fill my obligations as a citizen first and as a poet second. I had become paralyzed in terms of mobility and the freedom of expression, and I had become an easy morsel in the jaws of Israeli racism . . . The delicate thread of push and pull between me and Israeli law had snapped and my ability to evade, contrive, and prevail had come to an end" (Yaḥyá 2003, 167). We note here how strongly Darwish associated his sense of duty as a citizen with that of being a poet, and how the obstruction of the fulfillment of one duty equally affects the other.

Having examined Darwish's writings prior to his decision to leave Israel, we can see how his poetry was part of this push and pull between himself and Israeli society at large:

> They have taught me all the director's wishes—
> to dance to the beat of his lies.
> I'm tired now;
> my myths are hung out on a rope to dry . . .
>
> O my blood
> their brushes are drawing pictures of the Lidd region
> and you are their ink.
> Jaffa is nothing but the skin on their drums
> and my bones are like a bludgeon in the director's hand,

and I keep saying,
I'll perfect this role by tomorrow.
And so for this reason, I resign.

Ladies
and Gentlemen
I have entertained you for twenty years
and today it's time to leave,
time to escape this throng
and to sing in Galilee
to the sparrows that live in the nest of the impossible.
For this reason I resign,
resign,
resign.
(Darwish 2005, 321–22)

A sense of futility permeates this poem, titled "Wa yusdal al-sitar" (And the Curtain Falls). Here Darwish's speaker is a stage actor who has grown tired of his role and his audience. He had been merely an entertainment for them, having absorbed the role given to him but never having perfected it to the director's or the audience's satisfaction. He also feels that they are playing a kind of waiting game as they exploit him. They are busy claiming places that belong to him, inscribing them as their own, while using his labor to achieve their conquest. The speaker names Galilee as his destination, but in adding that it is "the nest of the impossible," we are unsure of where he will end up or what his fate will be.

In another poem of this period, Darwish expresses his deep sense of fatigue and exasperation when offering to exchange his love for his beloved and "the history of our ancestors" for "a day of freedom" (2005, 334). But with whom would he exchange it? Darwish's relationship with the Israeli readers had been complicated by the language barrier. Though not stated by Darwish, the dialogues that took place between Palestinian and Israeli writers were in Hebrew, while Darwish's articles and poems appeared in Rakah's Arabic publications. Only a few of his interviews appeared in Hebrew; in fact, throughout his career, his work was more available in languages other than in Hebrew (Shalat 1999, 153). The enemy with whom he wished to resolve his differences had refused to listen. The time had come for Darwish to leave Zion and to work on creating Palestine from outside the fortress walls.

Reconfiguring the Creative Process

In discussing "A Soldier Dreams of White Lilies," I noted how the poem manages to address Israeli, Palestinian, and Arab anxieties and concerns, and how the poem grants each of these audiences an array of elements to identify with while they are also forced to acknowledge the humanity of the Other. But what if this poem and others like it are not made available in the Other's language? What happens to the poet's interdependently connected process of gaining agency? What happens to the poet's process of writing when the circuit of poet/poem/reader is not completed?

These questions can perhaps be examined by referring to "Discourse in Life and Discourse in Poetry," an early essay by the Russian theorist Mikhail Bakhtin (1997) in which he outlines the social exchange that takes place in poetry between the poet, poet-speaker (protagonist), and the reader. Bakhtin assumes that the bond between the poet-speaker and the poet composing the poem is so strong that there is hardly "any distance between the poet and his discourse" (Todorov 1984, 65). Nonetheless, the poet, the reader, and the speaker of his poem are separate. Within the compositional process, the reader is someone who exists in the poet's imagination, as does the speaker of any poem. In other words, the poem is created in an internal space where these three forces combine and struggle to shape the poem as best as they know how. This threesome is *"part of an artistic event that has a particular social structure inspired by that very artistic act or event* . . . The [reader] we refer to is *a participant from inside* the artistic event and he is determined from within the form of the art work" (Todorov 1984, 59; italics mine). This reader and the speaker of a poem are not doppelgängers or lifelong imaginary friends of the poet, but they are people who emerge with the demands of a given poetic composition, a phase of writing, or a subject matter, and who are concerned with form and content. In other words, each poem creates its own ideal reader and speaker who change with the poet's circumstances and the formal and intellectual challenges he faces.

The point to make about Darwish's work here in regard to Bakhtin's theory of the creative process is that as Darwish left Israel/Palestine and became an exile first in Moscow, then Cairo, and Beirut, his circumstances and his sense of voice as a poet naturally had to change, as did the internal reader and poet-speakers of his poems.

Most important for Bakhtin in his outline of the compositional process is that the reader inside the poetic discourse must never be mixed up in any way or manner with the public, or real readers, who are and ought to remain totally outside the work and its creation: "If the poet's consciousness and consideration of the outside public begin to occupy an important role in the poet's work, the work will lose its artistic purity and will fall to a lower social level. When he begins to pay attention to outside factors, the poet then loses the listener that is closest to him [inside him] and he begins to break the social totality that the work of art has already configured within it" (Todorov 1984, 60). Bakhtin here is reiterating that a poetic discourse (the lyric poem) results from an internal dialogue between the poet, the speaker of the poem, and the poet's internal reader. The aforementioned attraction and struggle between these three consciences, if you will, take place within the poet. The poem is thus a social act, a dialogue that takes place within the poet as he internalizes various social, historical, and political developments that influence the creation of the poem.

Looking at Darwish's "Soldier"—and several poems from the late 1960s, such as "Imra'a Jamila fi Sadum" (A Beautiful Woman in Sodom), "Kitaba 'ala ḍaw bunduqiya" ("Writing in the Light of a Rifle"), and "Al-jissr" ("The Bridge")—we note that Darwish's sense of his potential reader expanded quite impressively since his earliest poems. He had continued to write within the contingencies of Palestinian experience and managed to create composite internal readers who are part Palestinian, part Arab, part Israeli, part victim, part victimizer, and part observer. These new internal readers transcend the poet's individual constituencies and perhaps approach the universal reader that the young Darwish addressed in his very first book and of whom he asked forgiveness for having to express his anger. However, as Darwish continued to develop various poet-speakers and to shape internal readers who would challenge him, the real readership—the public— was becoming increasingly divided over his role as a poet of the nation and chronicler of its triumphs and travails.

Psalmist of Exile

Poet of the Palestinian Diaspora

In 1971, after spending part of a year in Moscow, Darwish arrived in Cairo. A little more than a year later, he relocated to Beirut to join the Palestinian resistance "in the nest of the impossible" (2005, 322). As he began to travel extensively, Darwish's life changed from that of the confined poet who has to check into a police station in Haifa at sunset and spend the evening and night at home—and who is often denied permission to visit his family in the village of al-Jadida—to a poet who can feel the restlessness of displacement. Understandably, his subject matter also changed, if only due to his own new experiences.

Darwish's few travels out of Israel before he left in 1970 had been highly visible. A few years before deciding to leave, he and fellow poet Samih al-Qasim were caught up in a controversy in the Arab world for being part of an Israeli Communist youth delegation to Moscow. While in Moscow, he was a regular subject of interest to visiting Arab journalists and writers.

His decision to leave Israel was a headline-grabbing event. He was immediately embraced by the Palestine Liberation Organization (PLO) and welcomed to Cairo by high government officials. Nonetheless, many Palestinians objected and thought he would have been more effective had he remained inside Palestine/Israel. One important objection to Darwish's departure came from Ghassan Kanafani no less, who wrote a major article in the Lebanese weekly *Al-Ḥadith* (al-Naqqāsh 1971, 274). The Israeli Communist Party (Rakah), which Darwish belonged to, also issued a public statement, authored by Emile Habibi, expressing regret at having lost Darwish but also blaming the Israeli government for forcing his hand.

In moving to Cairo in 1971 and later to Beirut in 1973, Darwish transitioned from living in a deterritorialized community within the belly of the settler-colonial beast to the wide land-ocean of the Arab world; from working as an editor in a struggling publication to a regular contributor to the Arab world's largest and most influential newspapers; from being ignored and doubted by the people whom he most wanted to influence to being embraced by the "ruthless love" (Darwish 1971, 131) of an audience that had placed such high expectations on him; and finally, from being an activist in a fringe party to being a member of the political establishment, albeit of a beleaguered people. By the late 1960s, Darwish's books had been smuggled out of Israel, reprinted multiple times in Lebanon, and sold all over the Arab world.

During this period (1971–1986) Darwish's poetry becomes preoccupied with Palestinian life in the diaspora. Whereas the Palestinians in exile prefigured in his earlier poetry as "the banished"—with only snippets of their phone conversations heard or their letters quoted—they now become a major preoccupation of Darwish's. Continuing the experiments with dialogue and narrations that he utilized in "A Soldier Dreams of White Lilies," Darwish presents a character no less controversial and complicated than Sirhan Sirhan,

the Jordanian-born Palestinian American who assassinated
Senator Robert Kennedy in 1968, though the poem leaves
some room for speculation about its protagonist. In "Sirhan
yashrabu al-qahwa fi al-kafateria" ("Sirhan Drinks Coffee
in the Cafeteria") Darwish's protagonist, like the assassin
in real life, is a highly confused and enigmatic Palestinian
young man, made delusional by the loss of his homeland and
victimized by the disfiguration of his identity:

> And we wrap ourselves in your name [Palestine],
>   but it was not love.
> Two hands utter something, then their light goes out.
> And Sirhan lies when he says he suckled on your
>   [Palestine's] milk.
> Sirhan is the child of a travel ticket.
> He was raised in the kitchen of a ship that never sailed
>   your waters.
>   — What's your name?
>   — I forgot.
>   — What's your father's name?
>   — I forgot.
>   — Your mother's
>   — I forgot.
>   — Did you sleep well last night?
>   — I slept a lifetime.
>   — Did you dream?
>   — A lot.
>   — Of what?
>   — Of things I never saw in my life.
> Then he suddenly shouted at them:
>   — Why did you eat vegetables smuggled from the
> fields of Jericho?

— Why did you drink olive oil stolen from Christ's
wounds?
And Sirhan is accused of being a strange exception from
the norm. (2005, 2:99–100)

Sirhan is a motherless, fatherless murderer who dreams
of things he never saw in his life. His grievances of a lost
homeland and endless displacement have shaken his vision
of reality. In exile, the milk he never suckled and the waters
he never sailed haunt him. After what seems like a stupor
caused by shock and anguish, he lashes out at those who feed
on the nurturance of his homeland, from which he had been
orphaned.

In the poem "What Was to Happen Did Happen" (*Kana
ma sawfa yakun*), Darwish provides a tender, evocative portrait of his fellow Palestinian poet, Rashed Hussein, who, a
few years older than Darwish, was considered the leader of
the young Palestinian poets inside Israel. The poet-speaker
reunites with Hussein on Fifth Avenue in New York City
where, now "gray like the sun in the forest of concrete"
(2005, 2:248), Hussein had relocated, permanently barred
from returning to his homeland. A year later, Hussein visits the poet in Cairo, and after thirty minutes in the city he
says, "I wish I were as free / as I was in the Nazareth prison"
(251). The poem provides a heartbreaking portrait of the displaced poet-intellectual, banished from his language, from
his cause, and tragically, from poetry. This is what Hussein
says in Darwish's poem:

From café to café, I seek another language.
I seek the difference between memory and fire.

I seek the first frontier of my own limbs.
Give me my arm to embrace others.
Give me some wind so that I can walk.
From café to café,
why does poetry escape my heart the further
I travel away from Jaffa?
Why does Jaffa disappear when I embrace her?
This time is not my time . . .
. . . .
. . . .
This time is not my time.
No, this country is not my country.
No, this body is not my body. (250–51)

The first line of this passage echoes Darwish's own sense of
physical incapacitation in his last days in Israel. Hussein, as
represented in this poem, is not merely paralyzed; he has lost
his limbs and is roving from café to café unable to connect
with others, burned by his memories. Hussein is existentially
displaced by exile belonging to neither his time, nor the country he lives in, nor even to his own body.

Darwish devotes much of his poetry now to the Palestinian experience of exile. He returns to this subject matter and
language with greater depth and formal innovation in the following decades. What distinguishes Darwish's poetry of exile
in the early to mid-1970s is perhaps the distinction "between
memory and fire," (250) as the poem symbolizes the exile's
construction of his past and the anguish of his displacement.
This theme can be seen in poems such as "'Aidun ila Yaffa,"
("Returning to Jaffa"), "Al-madinah al-muḥtalah" ("The
Occupied City"), "Al-nuzul min al-karmal" ("Descending Mt.

Carmel"), and "Al-khuruj min saḥil al-mutawist" ("Leaving the Mediterranean Shore")—all lyric poems that evoke the homeland, its landscape, and its people and that repeatedly recall the burn of memory that spread across his exiled body.

Poems of Exodus

Poet of the Armed Struggle

During the bulk of the period from 1971 to 1986, we find Darwish in Beirut. His departure from Cairo in 1973 appears to have taken place without rancor between him and his Egyptian hosts. Cairo, at the time, was still the pan-Arab political capital, but the cultural dynamism and innovation radiated from Beirut. Most importantly, Beirut was then the headquarters of the Palestine Liberation Organization, along with other Palestinian political and militant organizations. From Beirut, Palestinians conducted armed resistance to Israel and pursued political efforts for statehood. Darwish quickly joined the PLO structure, directing one of its cultural research centers and editing the journal *Shu'un Filasṭiniya* (*Palestinian Affairs*). There he came into close contact with PLO leader Yasser Arafat, becoming one of his leading speechwriters. He is especially noted for writing Arafat's 1976 speech to the UN's General Assembly. Arriving in Beirut, Darwish was already considered "the poet symbol" (al-sha'ir al-rāmz) for his poetry written in Palestine. But the Beirut period, as Nazim al-Sayyid (2008) reports, was full of contention, since Darwish had to engage the complicated machinations and inside politics of the revolution.

The unofficial poet laureate of the Palestinian resistance when Darwish arrived in Beirut was Muʻim Bissisu, whom Darwish had to compete with to lead the cultural side of the Palestinian struggle. Arafat played the two poets off of each other, repeatedly siding with Darwish, but never diminishing Bissisu's power and influence (al-Sayyid 2008, 7). Needless to say, the tensions between the two poets grew heated, and because both accused the other of being Arafat's poetic mouthpiece, they derogatorily called each other "The Poet-in-Chief" (al-shaʻir al-ʻām), a play on Arafat's title "Commander-in-Chief" (7).

In Beirut, Darwish became a producer of what Barbara Harlow defined as resistance poetry in its strictest sense. According to Harlow, resistance poetry accompanies an armed struggle and is made up of poems "often composed on the battlefield or commemorating its casualties" (Harlow 1987, 35). Even while inside Israel, Darwish, as previously noted, supported the Palestinian armed struggle for territories occupied by Israel in the 1967 war. His poems, however, did not become directly identified with the Palestinian armed struggle. His first two volumes of poetry published after leaving Israel, *Uḥibuki aw lā Uḥibuki* (*I Love You or I Don't Love You*, 1972) and *Muḥāwala Raqam Sabʻa* (*Attempt Number Seven*, 1973), elegize victims of Israeli violence, but none are focused on the armed struggle or the figure of the Palestinian freedom fighter, the *fidaii*, who "leads his people to freedom, without himself participating in it" (Neuwirth 2008, 178). The celebration of the *fidaii* had been a popular subject matter for Arabic and Palestinian poetry, especially since the 1967 defeat, when it became clear that the only fight in the region would have to take place between Palestinians and Israelis, since all the Arab state armies had been trounced (Sulaiman 1984, 139). Darwish's poetry of this time concerns the freedom he had in choosing his approach to his subject matter and his obligation to remain steadfast and loyal to the struggle and its institutions.

Any conscious participant in such "collective and concerted struggle against hegemonic domination and oppression" (Harlow 1987, 29) where much was at stake would feel constrained about pointing to the movement's failings. But resistance movements would not be sustainable if participants did not point to these contradictions and if such criticism was not heeded. "It is precisely these self-critical controversies that sustain the movements' active agency in the historical arena of world politics," adds Harlow (29). Regarding the role of the poet as agent here—even according to Harlow's formulation of resistance literature—it is unclear whether poetry or literature as such can be part of that "self-critical process," or if poetry is reserved for "the arena of struggle" (Yaḥyá 2003, 198) against occupying and hegemonic forces.

Darwish's writing during the Beirut period makes it seem that he felt his poetry should be obliged to the arena of struggle. Two decades later, he would say that he felt a strong tension between the poet and the politician in him, a split that did not seem to exist when he lived in Israel. And when confronted in a 1999 interview by poet Ghassan Zaqtan, who accused him of catering to his audience and providing them with familiar subject matter and tone during the Beirut years, Darwish replies only that his poetry "stumbled during this period" (Darwish 1999a, 28) without giving any reasons why.

As a creative dilemma, and a crisis in poetic agency, the issue Darwish faced here can be understood within the Bakhtinian model of the creative social unit presented earlier. The difficulty is twofold. First, Darwish is addressing an audience that does not challenge him—and a fully accepting audience demands to be fed what it is used to and insists on being paid back for the unquestionable authority it has given the poet. Second, having become the recognized poet-symbol (al-sha'ir al-rāmz) of Palestine, Darwish has little room to maneuver between his public role as an official poet and the private voice of a lyric poet, albeit a poet who is deeply concerned about public matters. With this gap between an autobiographical private self and the public poetic self, the poet is forced to deliver an uncomplicated message—albeit with a complicated texture and with much prosodic innovation—due to the small creative space in which he is allowed to maneuver. In Bakhtin's terms, the poem's social unit available to Darwish ceased to be soundproof here. We cannot tell whether the poet is absorbing impressions of the world through his inner interlocutors and utilizing them for creative work or if he is directly responding to the dissonance penetrating his creative enclosure.

The complexity of Darwish's situation is best addressed by turning to poems from his Beirut period. In the poem "Ṭuba li sha'in la yaṣil" ("Praise for a Thing That Did Not Arrive"), Darwish celebrates Palestinian martyrs whose death he presents as an endless wedding procession:

This is the wedding that never ends
in a battlefield that has no end
on a night that never ends.
This is the Palestinian wedding

where lover never reaches beloved
except as a martyr or a refugee. (2005, 2:158)

Here Darwish participates in the then newly fashioned symbol of the martyr as groom, where a wedding, instead of a wake, is held for the martyred fighter or victim. According to Muhawi (2006), such mock weddings were traditionally given at the funeral of "a young man who died before he had the chance to get married and have children" (38). On the way to the mosque or church, the deceased young man is carried as in "a wedding procession, with *dabke* dancing and singing" (38). Most significantly, this ritual took place regardless of the manner of death and was practiced by both Muslims and Christians. For Muhawi, "the existential irony implied in this behavior is deeply rooted in Palestinian culture" (38).

As the Palestinian quest for self-determination began, this tradition was stripped of its existential irony, and the funeral of a young man who died at the hands of the enemy became a politically charged wedding. The martyred young man became groom to the feminized land for whose sake he died. Taking up this motif along with other poets such as Ahmad Daḥbour and Muʻim Bissisu, Darwish writes that the martyrs and their sacrifices are paving the path for Palestinians to return to their homeland:

Their blood is before me,
inhabiting the city that approaches us
as if their wounds are the ships of exodus,
except that they do not return . . .
Their blood is before me . . .
I cannot see it

as if it is my country
before me and I do not see it
as the roads of Jaffa, before me,
and I cannot see them
as if the red roof-tiles of Haifa—
I cannot see them,
as if all the homeland's windows
have disappeared inside my blood.
Only the martyrs can see . . .
Only they can see
because they have been released from the skin of defeat
and from mirrors.
Here they are flying about their old rooftops
like swallows, like shrapnel.
They are setting themselves free. (2005, 2:158–59)

Only the martyred ones are free and are capable of seeing the future, because they have been liberated from defeat. Neuwirth (2008) argues that such an embrace of the martyr is an "act of inventing sacred history: elevating the fighter to the rank of a redeemer figure" (178). She adds that Darwish was articulating the aspirations of "a decisive movement promising liberation, to live the miracle of an Exodus" (178). Darwish delivers this quasi-religious vision of the martyr without any hint of irony or doubt. "Only the martyrs can see," states the poet, declaring the failure of poetic vision and thus positioning the poet as a chronicler blindly serving the cause.

Muffled Epical Screams

Darwish's best-known poem celebrating the *fidaii* is "Aḥmad al-Zaʿtar," which appeared in the volume titled *Aʿras*

(*Weddings*, 1977). Framed within the martyrdom-wedding motif, the character of Aḥmad al-Za'tar brings forth Darwish's most ambitious articulation of Palestinian armed resistance. The poem's poet-speaker, whose voice often overlaps with al-Za'tar's, makes the poem seem like both a eulogy given before the dead al-Za'tar's body and a song of praise delivered to him while alive. Like the martyrs in the previously quoted poem, those who died for the homeland are not granted the afterlife of Islamic theology, but they nonetheless hover as benign spirits among the living. Al-Za'tar exists in the present tense: he is presently dead and alive, hero and victim, plaintiff and judge, and he promises justice.

Aḥmad al-Za'tar's name refers to Tel al-Za'tar (Hill of Thyme), a Palestinian refugee camp in Lebanon where Palestinians were massacred. Accusing the PLO of supporting their leftist adversaries, Lebanese Maronite Christian "Phalangist" forces began to target the largely underarmed Palestinian refugee camps and, in the spring of 1976, surrounded Tel al-Za'tar. After a seven-month siege, and with the aid of Syrian armed forces, Phalangist forces managed to break Palestinian resistance in the camp and kill 3,000 Palestinian refugees (Schultz 2003, 76–78).

The difficulty the poem "Aḥmad al-Za'tar" presents has to do with the limitations, if not self-censorship, it faces. The poem hardly addresses the reality of the Palestinian situation in Lebanon. Indeed, the poem does not address the specifics of the Tel al-Za'tar events or that they occurred in Lebanon to begin with. There is no date given to commemorate the siege or the massacre. Nor does the poem name the culprits—neither the Syrians nor the Phalangists. In his earlier poetic sequence, "Azhār al-damm" ("Flowers of Blood"),

Darwish commemorates the victims of the Kafr Qasim massacre of Palestinians by Israeli soldiers in 1956. We are given the number of the victims as well as information on the massacre's events. In "He Returned . . . in a Shroud," Darwish refuses to name the victims, only offering indicative titles. The same is true for the poems "Ḍaḥiya raqam 18" ("Victim No. 18") and "Ḍaḥiya raqam 48" ("Victim No. 48"). However, the victims in the earlier poems are presented as sons and brothers, mothers and daughters, and so on. Victim No. 48 was found "with coins in his pocket / a book of matches, and a travel pass / and some tattoos drawn on his forearm" (2005, 1:227).

None of this particularity is granted to Aḥmad al-Zaʿtar. The protagonist's common name, Aḥmad, suggests that he is a Palestinian everyman. In this case, we are given an established persona ready to be filled with all the symbolism we bring to it. As stated previously, in "And He Returned . . . in a Shroud," Darwish refused to name his victims so their essence could remain in the details and so they "are not lost in the forest of names" (2005, 1:27). Now he offers us a name of a hero that stands for all the names, perhaps blocking them. Al-Zaʿtar, we learn from the poem, is self-sufficient and godlike: "His mother gave birth to him and withdrew" (2005, 2:259). "He grew as a refugee camp, blooming into thyme and freedom fighters" (260). A male fighter, al-Zaʿtar replaced his mother's withdrawal by becoming mother to other fighters and to the vegetation that surrounds the camp. "Alone, O how alone was Aḥmad"; he seeks an identity and is "flung by a volcano" (260). Al-Zaʿtar's life seems to be a cycle of these great triumphs coupled with tragic events brought on by betrayal.

In the first stanza that follows, Al-Za'tar reaches a moment of spiritual union with the land, much like the biblical Joseph, who has a dream granting him a high place among God's creatures. This realization of a special gift, in the cases of both Al-Za'tar and Joseph, is followed by betrayal by jealous, murderous brothers:

> I am the land and here it has come
> and dressed itself in me.
> I am the endless return to the homeland
> and I found myself filled with myself . . .

> From the Atlantic Ocean to the Arabian Gulf
> they were counting spears
> while Aḥmad climbed to see Haifa
> and he leapt.
> Now Aḥmad is the captive.
> The city left its streets
> and came toward him
> to kill him.
> From the Atlantic Ocean to the Arabian Gulf
> they were preparing the guillotine.
> They held an election for the sharpest blade.

> I am Aḥmad the Arab—let the siege come.
> My body is the walls—let the siege come.
> I am the edge of fire—let the siege come.
> And I now besiege you with my besiegement,
> I now besiege you
> and my chest is the door to all the world's people—
> let the siege come. (261–62)

The Palestinian fighter is the embodiment of the land, and he is the dream of the return of the homeland. In his mission and abidance to the land—as well as in the land's reliance on him—Ahmad finds his identity.

The Palestinian Ahmad is working toward regaining his homeland; he is leaping "to see Haifa." This is when his Arab brothers, from the Atlantic Ocean to the Persian Gulf, betray him and prepare their spears to upend him. Ahmad "the Arab" will survive, as he is the true link between the Arab masses. As for his betrayers, he will besiege them with the siege they have imposed upon him.

With its use of repetition and turns of phrase, "Ahmad al-Za'tar" exemplifies Darwish's turn toward the *nashid* (an anthem-like song), where ideas circulate and repeat musically, accruing in emotional resonance with less focus on narrative or rhetorical arcs. Reading the poem, we are nonetheless struck by the discrepancy between the desperate situation the Palestinians found themselves in at the time of this massacre and the poem's grandiloquent resonances. Bridging the poem's sonorous, uplifting rhythm with the facts one knows of Tel al-Za'tar makes for a difficult exercise in the suspension of disbelief.

Darwish, it should be noted, was considered part of the Palestinian political establishment at this time. His poems up to this point refer in passing to his disappointment with "the brothers," but in "Ahmad al-Za'tar" his self-imposed gag order becomes suffocating. Darwish clearly felt that the killings at Tel al-Za'tar deserved a response, and one that would take all the artist's capacities to honor the event. Whereas in Israel Darwish names his victimizer, here we detect political machinations and self-censorship at play for fear that some, even within the Palestinian camp, would be offended by what might be an undermining of Arab solidarity.

In 1983, after a silence of six years, and one year after the PLO's withdrawal from Beirut, Darwish published a book-length poem titled *Madih al-dil al-ʿali: Qaṣida tasji-liyah (Praise of the High Shadow: A Documentary Poem).* The withdrawal of the Palestinian resistance from Beirut was such a great blow to the Palestinian cause that Tel al-Zaʿtar pales before it in comparison. Israel occupied half of Lebanon for three months in 1982, and its march of devastation descended upon Beirut with fury. They bombed the city from land, air, and sea, causing the death of 19,000 civilians (Khalidi 1986, 200). The PLO negotiated a withdrawal of their fighters in August of that year, leaving Palestinian refugee camps vulnerable. In coordination with the Israeli invading forces, Phalangist militias descended upon the Sabra and Shatila refugee camps, murdering an estimated 2,000 Palestinian civilians. Darwish's poetic response to the Israeli invasion of Beirut, the civilian killings, and the massacres that followed differed only slightly in terms of form and approach from his work five years earlier. In *Praise of the High Shadow* we come across many echoes of "Aḥmad al-Zaʿtar":

> Besiege your besiegement, no way out.
> Your arms fell, pick them up.
> Strike your enemy, no way out. (2005, 2:348)

The lines are shorter, as if indicating the smaller space allowed for heroism. The repetition of phrases, such as "no way out" and "Either you are / or you shall not become" (349), occurs frequently and in close proximity to create a sense of aural claustrophobia. They are chants to help those addressed by the poem survive, but they also indicate the dire predicament in which the poet finds himself. Parts of *Praise of the High Shadow* are devoted to Beirut, where the poet speaks in We for the Palestinians addressing the paralyzed Arab brothers and the people of Lebanon. The poet feminizes Beirut and speaks to her as a lover. He later relays his dismay that she has betrayed him so blatantly. Beirut, described as the legendary female lover Laila, had always "refused to surrender to the husband" (2005, 2:365). She and the poet, standing in for the Palestinians, "were a life-boat for a continent floating on a mirage" (352), a reference to how the Palestinian cause had been a central component of the Arab postcolonial renaissance. Beirut was home to many publishing houses, newspapers, and theaters that rallied around the Palestinian cause, helping give shape to its progressive and liberal milieu. As such, the pro-Palestinian intellectual and artist, as well as the pro-Palestinian fighter (neither of which were always Palestinian), were Beirut's righteous and romantic suitors whose union bore the promise of Arab cultural rejuvenation. Now, however, "Beirut leaves the poet's poem / and enters the soldier's helmet" (369), a reference to the collaboration of many Lebanese with Israel, or at least the welcoming attitude some expressed toward the withdrawal of the Palestinians from Lebanon. Darwish also notes how Beirut had decided to embrace the petrodollars of the reactionary and philandering Arab princes. The feminized Beirut in *Praise of the High Shadow* proves to be a treacherous lover who betrays him outright, unlike Rita—the Israeli conscript—who at least demurs, and certainly unlike Palestine who remains faithful, for whose embrace he still longs.

"Aḥmad al-Zaʿtar" and *Praise of the High Shadow* have been considered lyric-epics by Arab critics such as Nāṣir (2001), Al-Ḥāj Ṣaleḥ (1999), and Al-Nabūlsī (1987). The poems are perhaps epical only in their size and in their focus on a hero, as is to be expected in the classical definition of an epic. Significantly, however, they lack the inclusive narrative and the clarity of purpose that chronology and an understanding of conflict require. Called "a documentary poem," *Praise of the High Shadow* is long on bombast and short on documentation. As in "Al-Zaʿtar," only snippets of the experience of that siege appear in the poem. The poem is a monologue directed at an agreeable, unskeptical listener, and both know the circumstances at hand. To know what the poem is about, anyone outside this closed conversation would have to bring to it, in terms of facts, much more than it offers us to weigh them. The musicality of *Praise of the High Shadow*, emphasized through incantation and repetition, rises into a kind of high shadow that neither the poet nor the reader can surmount. Trapped within a poetic discourse that promises documentation but cannot deliver, the poet circles around obscure images and dives into the self. "Go into yourself, / you are wider than people's lands, / wider than the width / of the guillotine blade" (2005, 2:391). Perhaps what the poem documents more than anything is the impossibility in that moment for the poet to "document." A host of reasons cause this impediment, one of which is the fact that Darwish's poetry at that time was read as quasi-official statement, a mode that does not allow the poet free reign and that forces him to write with the shadow of such implications hovering over him.

Most writers and poets from the region have long exercised a form of self-censorship, and central to this practice of self-censorship is the ability to subvert as well as acquiesce. In other words, the poet under self-censorship can manage to express the self and also satisfy the censor. In Darwish's case here, the censor—an internal and internalized one—proved stronger than the self. One may even argue that "Aḥmad al-Zaʿtar" and *Praise of the High Shadow* are poems about what the Palestinian intellectual/politician could not say by saying so much. Such external pressure on poetry, where the poet must withhold what he or she knows, and where his or her concern for not offending overwhelms his or her ability to express, makes for difficult reading, especially given the highly dramatic nature of the poem.

Adding to the poems' shortcomings is their very content which, in both cases, is focused on a single hero who boldly resisted, rather than a whole community victimized and blindsided by betrayal. *Madiḥ* was quickly perceived as indeed a *madiḥ* (panegyric ode) of Yasser Arafat for enduring this challenge to his leadership, a charge that Darwish had to repeatedly deny (Yaḥyá 2003, 200). It did not help the poem's reputation or Darwish's that he read it in public as Arafat gleefully listened (Ibrahim 2005, 16).

Prose Rescues Poetry

Poetic agency derives its discursive thrust from the versatility of the poet to change his timbre and approach to his subject, and thus changes the type of poem he writes. The aim of the poet-agent, as Darwish understood so well, is to be engaged and to help facilitate change. This process involves bearing witness through poetry, rewriting history, and challenging or affirming given concepts by confronting them or retooling them. One of the means also available to the poet is to acknowledge the failure of poetry in addressing a subject matter and to turn the material over to another genre. One of Darwish's significant revelations after Beirut is perhaps encapsulated in the title of his poem "It Is Time for the First Lines to Die" (2005, 3:72). By that we may understand that the poet's projected persona and the role he had assumed have reached their creative ends after Beirut. The poet-Darwish needed to be reborn if he was to remain relevant and alive as a poet. Announcing the death of the poet he had been and the discursive approach he had been practicing up to that point, Darwish acknowledges the need for a new method of writing poetry.

We have already discussed the generic division of labor in Palestinian literature between poetry and prose, where factual, realist material found its way to prose fiction and the visionary and dramatic expressed itself in poetry. Darwish's prose memoir, *Ḏākirah lil-nisyān* (*A Memory for Forgetfulness*), first published 1984, seems an acknowledgment of this division, as well as an assertion of the beginning of individual and national self-examination. Here we find the Darwish of *Praise of the High Shadow* stripped of elevated eloquence. At times, his descent is like Shakespeare's Othello in the latter half of the play. Foul-mouthed, loquacious, and suffering from lack of sleep, Darwish's protagonist in *A Memory for Forgetfulness* is free to tell it like it is. We read about him and friends scrounging for food, one of them carrying a lamb carcass hoping to find a place to cook it. "Why don't you take this thing, poke a hole in it, and fuck it, I told him," he writes

(2007, 79). A remarkable passage describes the poet's effort to try to cross a small hallway in his apartment to make his morning coffee in the midst of intense bombing. Unlike Othello, however, Darwish is clear-eyed about the experience he is narrating. He presents his Lebanese neighbor's disdain of the Palestinians with little interference. And in the midst of the painful silence of the Arab governments, he finds ironic hope in the protests that broke in several Arab cities when the Algerian national team was treated unjustly at the 1982 World Cup that summer in Spain.

Darwish's account of the Israeli occupation of Lebanon, specifically its bombardment of civilians and the siege of Beirut, attempts to inscribe what would otherwise be lost to forgetfulness, such as "events that collective and cultural memory, let alone history, can't bring themselves to say" (Bernard-Donals 2009, 42). We might add poetry to "collective and cultural memory" and "history" here, since it is prose that enables Darwish to demystify the complexity of the Palestinian situation in Beirut. In *A Memory for Forgetfulness*, the major actors appear under their own names (Arafat, Begin, Sharon, Jemayael, Saad Haddad, and so on). Whereas in "Aḥmad al-Zaʿtar" and *Praise of the High Shadow* Darwish had drowned the complexity with accusations of betrayal directed at the Arab capitals, here we learn of the depth of the Palestinian tragedy. Working as clients of Arab regimes that wished to be seen as champions of the struggle for Palestine, many Palestinian leaders were instrumental in sapping their own national liberation movements. Darwish reiterates his praise for the Palestinian *fidaii*, and his celebration here counteracts the lyricism of his previous grandiloquent portrayals. The fighters, we learn, were short on ammunition, water, and food; yet through their tactical cunning and perseverance, they forced the Israelis to stay on the fringes of the city.

Though it does a much better job at documenting Palestinian experience in Beirut than *Praise of the High Shadow*, *A Memory for Forgetfulness* is also tasked with attempting to assure the Palestinians of their cultural and national relevance past the Lebanon experience. In Beirut's Commodore Hotel, where opportunists, hedonists, and adventurers hid during the war, Darwish has this conversation with an American journalist:

> —What are you writing now, poet?
> —I am writing my silence.
> —Do you mean that only the guns are talking now?
> —Yes, their voice is louder than mine.
> —So what are you doing?
> —I am encouraging people to persevere.
> —Will you win this war?
> —No. What's important is that we survive. Our survival is victory.
> —And what happens after that?
> —A new time will begin.
> —And when will you return to writing poems?
> —After the guns fall quiet for a bit. Then I can explode my silence, which is filled with all these voices.
> (2007a, 65)

Here Darwish already has a sense that a new era is emerging and a new poetry needs to emerge with it. He quotes passages from his poetry, citing these previously discussed lines in *Praise of the High Shadow* and describing his writing as "the stutters of a scream" (2007, 61). In providing this critique of *Praise of the High Shadow*, Darwish manages to stitch these stutters into lucid prose, suggesting that what was needed for him as a poet-agent is a degree of sobriety rather than the exhilaration of battle-born poetry.

Furthermore, Darwish's incorporation of long passages from the ancient books of the three major monotheist religions in *A Memory for Forgetfulness* hint at the ingredients of a new mythology of Palestine. Darwish also turns to history, digging through chronicles of the Crusades for parallels to his Beirut experience. The Crusades prove to be a rich resource for studying a prolonged state of ambivalence, displacement, and disorientation. This focus on mythology, history, and the machinations of survival indicate that Darwish's imagination, even while in Beirut, was already refashioning the inner interlocutors of his creative process in preparation for launching a new era in Palestinian culture and the poetic articulation it would require.

5

To Survive in the World

Writing the Deep Present and the Deep Past, 1986–1993

Having worked within the framework of *adab al-iltizam* (committed literature), but with rising misgivings about "a poetry that ignites revolution" (Darwish 1979, 184) Darwish faced a new chapter in the Palestinian saga and a new challenge to his ideas about poetry as a means of agency for poet and reader. Like many Palestinian intellectuals in the mid-1980s, Darwish seems to have recognized that the fight for Palestinian statehood and self-determination had to take on a more varied, strategic, long-term course of action. Palestinian writers and poets began to sense that their literature, their internal debates, and even their cultural negotiations with the enemy would also have to take place on the global stage. By the time Beirut fell in 1982, many Palestinians had realized the durability of Zionist ideology and its ability to dominate the fate of Palestine. Steeped in biblical mythology, but taken as history, the Zionist vision of Palestine contributed, at least within global circles of power, to tacit acceptance of the Palestinians' suffering and marginalization. Now that the military option had become almost moot, the battle for

Palestinian statehood, as far as the exiled Palestinians were concerned, would take place in the cultural arena as well as the political one. Within the arts, the Palestinians' struggle would depend on providing compelling portraits and metaphors for their suffering, replacing propaganda with artistry and intellectual rigor. This process would require the development of diverse visions of a peaceful future for Palestinians and Israelis, and it would aim to destabilize the entrenched racist paradigms legitimizing Palestinian displacement and suffering since the establishment of Israel on their historical homeland.

Toward this end, two books that are now considered masterpieces of Palestinian literature were published—one in Arabic and one in English: Mahmoud Darwish's poetry collection *Wardun Aqall* (*Lesser Roses*, 1986) and Edward Said's *After the Last Sky: Palestinian Lives*. Said's book significantly takes its title from a line that appears in *Lesser Roses*. Said acknowledges Darwish's involvement in *After the Last Sky* and intersperses his texts with lines from *Lesser Roses*. The extent to which Darwish and Said worked together on these two projects may never be determined, but it is evident that the books were written around the same time and can be read as a unified project. Together they point the way toward new aesthetics in Palestinian art and a new approach to the role of art in both the development of Palestinian culture and the advocacy of the Palestinians' cause.

Said's introduction to *After the Last Sky* provides what amounts to a national cultural agenda that Palestinian artists, within the homeland and without, have largely adhered to ever since. Said's prescriptions are informative in outlining Darwish's new direction as a poet.

Said shifts the focus of the Palestinian fight for recognition toward the West, especially toward the United States, where the Palestinians—realizing they lost their public relations battle to the Israelis and their supporters—must combat their image as terrorists (Said 1999, 4). The Palestinians' affiliation with and reliance on their Arab brothers has brought them a great deal of grief, and the time has come for the Palestinians to take matters (political, social, and cultural) fully into their own hands.

Said's condemnation of violence covers that committed by the Israelis, their allies, and the Palestinians. The violence most harmful to Palestinians has been that "wreaked upon each other" (1999, 5). In its condemnation of violence, Said's aesthetic program implies that the Palestinians' armed resistance, and even the political processes involved in seeking a Palestinian state, should become less central as a focal point of Palestinian self-presence in the world. Despite their decades-long hardship and their "various and scattered experiences" (Said 1999, 5), the Palestinians have formed a community that embraces their multiple affiliations, histories, and backgrounds. Their arts therefore seek to represent this diversity through "unconventional, hybrid, and fragmentary forms of expression" (6).

Palestinians should be encouraged to have their conversations with the world and among themselves in public, through art and literature. Consequently, Palestinian artwork should be made available everywhere possible, and Palestinian literature should be made readily available through translation (Said 1999, 7).

Just as the intifada was about to ignite, the late 1980s saw increased exposure of Palestinian art and literature in the West. Darwish's relocation to Paris facilitated the translation of more of his work into French and other Western European languages; Michel Khleifi's feature film "Wedding in Galilee" won the Critics Prize at the Cannes Film Festival in 1987; and Anton Shammas's novel *Arabesques*, the first novel written in Hebrew by a non-Jew, in fact by a Palestinian, caused a huge stir in Israeli cultural circles and among American Jewish intellectuals. *Arabesques* was recognized for its literary excellence by leading Israeli critics and was translated into many languages. A few years later, the renowned Palestinian scholar Salma Khadra Jayyusi published her voluminous *Anthology of Palestinian Literature*, thus canonizing a national body of work. Significantly, Jayyusi's anthology appeared in English several years before it appeared in Arabic, suggesting that this canonization of Palestinian national literature was an outward gesture and that, indeed, Palestinian culture was shaping itself, forming its identity, before the eyes of the world.

Collective Soliloquies

In *Lesser Roses*, Darwish begins by responding to a poem in his previous book *Hiya Ughnia, Hiya Ughnia* (*It's a Song, It's a Song*, 1985), which he ended with the startling declaration, "It's time for the poet to kill himself / not for anything, / but to kill himself" (2005, 3:75). In *Lesser Roses*, the poet begins with a vow "to walk this long, long road to its end" (107), convinced that "in this life there is much to love" (111). Darwish's embrace of life is coupled with an embrace of poetry as he emerges a new poet with a new look to his poems. Armed with formal innovations and speaking in a more immediate, wide-reaching timbre, Darwish returns forcefully to language because "it is all he has recourse to . . . eager to show that as a poet he cannot be but a poet" (Snir 2008, 126).

The titles of the poems in *Lesser Roses* are usually the first few words of the poem. It is common for poems to be known for their first lines, but not to be titled as such. With titles that do not encapsulate or shed a retrospective light, the poems gush forth as whole utterances until they reach their end. This immediate leap into the poems' content is marked by the absence of sections or stanzas in the vast majority of the book, as if there is no time to pause. Shifts in rhetoric, focus, or subject matter within the poems have to be taken as part of the whole and are indicative of the turbulence of the moment experienced.

Lesser Roses, as a volume, contrasts with Darwish's foray into the lyric-epics of Beirut. Most of the poems occupy a single page and are written in long lines—suggestive of "the long, long road" that the poem, and the poet, must walk. This combination, of long lines in short poems, is new to Darwish. And the fact that the poems are all of similar length suggests that, in many ways, they are a studied variation on a theme. The settings of the poems—Córdoba, Aden, and others—change, but the circumstances remain similar. Repeatedly, we find ourselves caught within the same prolonged delay, mired in the hurry-up-and-wait of the Palestinian exilic experience. Several poems employ rhyme, but unlike the variations on rhyme that Darwish and other *taf'ila* poets had used, in *Lesser Roses* he typically uses only a single rhyming sound. Darwish's lines are longer even than the *bahr al-ṭawil* (long measure, or foot) lines of classical poetry, which can contain up to twenty syllables in Arabic. The combination of very long lines with a monorhyme scheme provides a looping track that lands us back where we started, caught up in a cycle of repeated sounds, perhaps learning a great deal, but making little physical progress.

In *Lesser Roses*, we sense that Darwish is addressing a different reader and has to start off with a clean referential slate. The poems in *Lesser Roses* do not require the reader to share the poet's past or know a great deal of history, since whatever history the poet refers to here is made explicit in the poems. Instead, the poems attempt to establish a relationship with the reader by anchoring themselves in the elements, reaching a point of agreement and moving on from there. Darwish's poem "Fi hadhih al-arḍa ma yastaḥiqu al-ḥayah" ("On This Earth There Is What Deserves Life") is a case in point:

On this earth there is what deserves life: April's hesitancy,
    the smell of bread
at dawn, a woman's invocation toward men, Aeschylus's
    writings, the beginning
of love, grass on a stone, mothers standing on a thread
    issued from the notes of a flute,
and the conqueror's dread of memories.

On this earth there is what deserves life: the end of
    September, a woman who leaves
her forties with her apricots still in bloom, the hour of
    sun in the prison yard, clouds
imitating a herd of creatures, the salutations given to
    those who walk smiling
to their executions, and the tyrants' fear of songs.

On this earth there is what deserves life: on this earth
    there is the mistress of
the earth, mother of beginnings and mother of ends. She
    used to be called Palestine.
And she is still called Palestine. My lady, I deserve,
    because you are my lady, I deserve life. (2005,
    3:111–12)

In the first two stanzas, Darwish begins by trying to reach consensus with the reader. The first reason to live he mentions is April's hesitancy, an observation about nature and climate that humans must have observed before any civilization came into being. Then he cites the smell of bread at dawn, which ties the joys of food with the exhilaration of early morning and the satisfaction of fulfilling labor. A woman's invocation toward a man combines the worlds of desire and superstition. As soon as he mentions Aeschylus's writings, the poet-speaker realizes he may have made a complex allusion, a point that would not be immediately clear to the reader, and he quickly returns to recognizable experiences, such as the beginning of love and the beautiful, yet incongruous image of grass growing on a stone.

The speaker saves the images more pertinent to the Palestinian experience for the last line in the first stanza, though Palestine itself gets no mention. Indeed, the image of mothers standing on a thread of anxiety, their sense of hope as fragile and whispery as the notes of a flute, offers a primordial anxiety with universal resonance. Finally, Darwish's poet-speaker asserts that the conqueror dreads his memories of conquest, because they evoke acts of violence and perhaps

Eliot

guilt. More importantly, the conqueror dreads the memory of the conquered because it fuels their resistance. They are two contrary drives—the drive to protect and the drive to dominate—and most people have experienced at least one of them. After listing reasons to live that many can identify with, Darwish inches closer toward the reasons Palestinians alone know more deeply.

The second stanza follows a similar pattern. The images of "the end of September" and "a woman who leaves her forties with her apricots still in bloom" as reasons to go on living should cause no confusion in the reader; both of these autumnal images celebrate beauty's ability to survive. In "the hour of sun in the prison yard," the poet inches closer to his people's experience, as detention and imprisonment by Israeli authorities were the fate of thousands of Palestinian men and women. Perhaps fearing he has gotten too specific, the poet veers back to "clouds imitating a herd of creatures," a pleasure associated with childhood anywhere. The stanza concludes with the political image of fearless heroes facing execution and a tyrant's fear of popular sentiment as expressed in song. These images are not particular to the Palestinians, but are easily associated with Palestine.

Darwish subtly embeds his own memories and his earlier poetry in the images of this poem. The smell of bread and the image of the anxious mother are part of Darwish's autobiographical references, especially "My Mother," which is one of his best-known compositions. Grass growing on a stone echoes Darwish's protagonist, Aḥmad al-Zaʿtar, who is described in these very terms. And finally, the hour of sun in the prison yard evokes Darwish's own imprisonments in

Israel. By inserting the Palestinian experience within the universal joys and achievements of life, Darwish presents himself as "synecdoche . . . of an entire people" (Snir 2008, 127) and, indeed, the whole of humanity.

In the third stanza, we realize the poet has saved his best reason to live for last. It is his country, of course. He has shown us that he and we have a great deal in common, and he has carefully brought us to the experience of his people. Whenever he senses that we may not agree with him, he presents more points that implicate us in the poem's search for existential affirmation. When he finally mentions Palestine, he presents it not as merely one more thing that makes life worth living, but as a special being, place, and entity—a woman perhaps foreshadowed by the woman who has maintained her beauty after decades of being longed for.

At the end of the poem, we realize that the poet may have not been speaking to us at all, but was speaking to his beloved lady/homeland all along. We have merely been given the privilege of overhearing this intimate declaration of love. This pleasurable destabilization places us momentarily outside of the poem, but through identification with the poet-speaker, we are compelled, in order to reenter the poem, to give serious consideration to his adoration for his homeland.

Darwish continues these inclusive gestures when he begins to speak in the first-person plural. The poems in *Lesser Roses* have no hesitancy about speaking in We, their confidence arising from the urgency of the situations described as they encapsulate the moment of an identity's birth. We see before us the evolution of a new Palestinian identity, a new "positioning," to use Stuart Hall's term (1996, 401). This reshaped identity, as expressed in Darwish's poems, is "constructed through memory, fantasy, narrative, and myth" (Hall 1994, 395) like all identities, but since this identity requires that the world witness its emergence, it relies more strongly on metaphor and sharp imagery as a means of dissolving the reader/viewer's skepticism and defensiveness.

Metaphor, as in the poem "Taḍiqu bina al-arḍ" ("Earth Is Pressing against Us") tells the Palestinians' "story" to others, and to themselves, in a much more urgent and existentially explicit manner than their "history" could:

> Earth is pressing against us, trapping us in the final
> passage, so we pull off our limbs to make it through.
> Earth is squeezing us. If only we were its wheat, so that
> we die then live. If only it were our mother
> so she might have mercy on us . . .
> Where do we go after the last frontier? Where do birds fly
> after the last sky?
>
> Where will plants sleep after the last breath of air? We
> will write our names with crimson
> mist! We will cut off the hymn's hand so that our flesh
> completes it.
>
> Here we will die. Here, in the final passage. Here or
> there, our blood will plant its olive trees. (2005,
> 3:115–16)

The questions at the center of this poem have a dramatic quality. Darwish starts the poem by making a case through metaphor. If the reader does not understand how hard life has been for the Palestinians, how their movement as individuals and as a community has been constricted, let the reader then imagine having to tear off his or her limbs in order to keep moving. The culprit is not a single enemy here, but the whole earth. Life under such pressure is so difficult that the poet wishes that he or his people were wheat so this life would end and they could start again. Life, therefore, takes priority over one's background or history, and the desire to live is itself more powerful than the desire to live as a human being.

No such option is available, however, and it is at this point that the poem turns to the reader and asks powerful questions: now that you understand our situation, through metaphor and analogy, and now that it has been presented to you in sharp, crisp images, what do you suggest we do, dear reader? With the apostrophic and repeated use of the word *here*, the reader is pulled deeper into the poem by the immediacy of the poet's utterance. Before the reader can answer the poet's questions, the world continues to press the people depicted in the poem, and they are forced to respond. They write their names with the blood of their massacred bodies; they attach their corpses to a severed song to complete it. And when their bodies are all bled out, their blood will plant its olive trees—a powerful symbol of peace, and a metaphor for Palestinian resilience and endurance.

Whereas "The Earth Is Pressing against Us" provides a metaphorical portrait of the Palestinians' agony, Darwish's "Athens Airport" brings the reader closer to their concrete reality:

Athens airport disperses us to other airports. Where can
I fight, asks the fighter. Where can I deliver your child?
a pregnant woman shouts back. Where can I invest my
money? asks the banker. This is none of my business, the
intellectual says. Where did you come from? asks the cus-
toms official. And we answer: From the sea! Where are
you going? To the sea, we answer. What is your address?
A woman of our group says: My village is my bundle on
my back. We have waited in the Athens airport for years.
A young man marries a girl but they have no place for their
wedding night. He asks: Where can I make love to her?
We laugh and say: This is not the right time for that question. The analyst says: In order to live, they die by mistake.
The literary man says: Our camp will certainly fall. What
do they want from us? Athens airport welcomes its visitors without end. Yet, like the benches in the terminal, we
remain, impatiently waiting for the sea. O Athens airport,
how many more years will this waiting take? (2005, 3:120)

As in the early poem "Identity Card," Darwish takes a fact
from his autobiography and enlarges his voice to become others'. Here we have a poem borne of Darwish's personal experience. In his letters to Samih al-Qasim, he makes references
to meeting old friends while in transit between flights—
people he never expected to see again. "Athens Airport"
points directly to the Palestinian situation after the PLO's
expulsion from Beirut in 1982 by including a fighter in the
crowd of waiting Palestinians. The fighter's presence among
the stranded travelers suggests that the armed facet of the
Palestinian struggle is on hold, as was the case in the mid-
1980s, at least as far as the PLO was concerned. The trauma

of separation and discontinuity unfolds very quickly as the fighter's wife has nowhere to bear her child, the banker has nowhere to invest his money, and so on.

It is important to note how the Palestinians are presented as "normal" in this poem. They represent various professional classes, which are the type of people we would see at an airport. The liminal condition of the Palestinians is expressed in the image of the woman who says that her bundle is her village. In her character, Darwish preserves the Palestinians' peasant roots; the traveling village woman has become a cosmopolitan traveler but still considers the village her basic social unit. Furthermore, Darwish's reference to her village celebrates a long-held tradition among displaced Palestinians of naming their ancestral villages (most of which no longer exist) when they are asked about their origins.

The Palestinians' existential sense of irony, as Muhawi (2006) called it, appears here too. The crowd waiting at the airport finds humor in the dilemma of the newlyweds, whose wedding itself was held at the airport. But gravity soon returns to the poem, and the poet turns to the reader, wondering what the world wants from him and his people, and how long this waiting will go on.

In another poem, Darwish's poet-speaker directly addresses an international gathering:

And I ask you kind ladies and gentlemen, is this people's
    earth for all of the earth's people? . . .
Where is my small hut then, where am I? . . .
You have all agreed to our right to return like all hens
    and horses to a dream of stone . . .

but I continue to travel on to another country,
so that I ask you again, kind ladies and gentlemen, is this
   people's earth for all of the earth's people? (2005,
   3:121–22)

This last passage makes explicit the kind of stage on which
Darwish is performing his poetry, and on which the Palestinian experience has been dramatizing itself before the world
audience. Now that the Palestinians' case has been made
with images, metaphors, and in dramatic representations
that can be easily understood, Darwish, again speaking in
We, directly challenges the global community's nonchalance
and urges his reader toward fairness.

The Battle over Myth and History

Earlier in his career, Darwish had argued that his and his
people's sense of belonging to Palestine differs from that of
the Israeli occupiers. Palestinians belong to Palestine and
their belonging does not have to be "excavated" (Darwish
1971, 8) to be proven. Their presence is rooted in their peasant traditions and in the lives they have been shaping on the
land, not in dreams or myths. He asserted that Israelis suffer
from their lack of belonging. His soldier who dreams of white
lilies says that his love for Israel was retrieved "from old ruins
. . . an old statue lost in time . . . an unknown source" (2005,
1:111). "A Soldier Dreams of White Lilies" forcefully suggests that Israelis have a great deal to learn from the Palestinians about loving one's homeland and belonging to it, as

their attachment does not compare to the Palestinians', and that violence against the native inhabitants alienates, rather than contributes to, one's sense of belonging to a place and its history.

The main textual source of the Israelis' sense of entitlement to Palestine is the Hebrew Bible rather than a deeply felt experience of the land and the life it bears. Israel established itself as a modern, democratic, secularly managed state for Jews, but with the Bible at the center of its legitimacy. And though most of the early Zionist leaders, including Herzl and Ben-Gurion, were skeptics, if not nonbelievers, the Bible is nonetheless at the center of the Zionists' claim on Palestine and has guided their approach to and treatment of the land's native inhabitants. Like the other European national movements in the nineteenth century by which it was inspired, the evolution of Zionism involved the invention of tradition, the creation of a modern national culture, and the construction of national identities from a mixture of folk history and historical myth (Hobsbawm 1990).

As a colonial movement, Zionism intended to settle European-born Jews in historical Palestine even at the expense of the land's native inhabitants. The Hebrew Bible helped define their parameters; in this case the national collectivity was to be made up of only ethnic Jews, including Jews all over the world, and was instrumental in positioning Palestinians as indisputable Others, whose presence on the land was undesirable. Jewish tradition and the Bible provided symbols for the new Jewish nation-state, including a national language—Hebrew—which was not a modern language and therefore needed to be secularized and transformed (Masalha 2007,

21–22). Most importantly, the Hebrew Bible was to serve as a cornerstone of Zionist political ideology and governance.

Israeli historian Baruch Kimmerling (1999) writes: "The book of Joshua provided the muscular and militaristic dimension of conquest of and annihilation of the Canaanites and other ancient people that populated the Promised Land, while the Books of Isaiah and Amos were considered as preaching for social justice and equality (a kind of proto-socialism)" (339).

As the Zionist movement evolved from its early stages of drawing on biblical sources to construct its national vision and character, it began to assert the biblical myth as valid history, whereby "the Bible became the warrant for possession of the land" (Biale 2010, 86). This was in keeping with other efforts in the West aimed at validating the historicity of the Bible. These efforts, both religious and secular, penetrated many fields of study, especially archeology. During much of the twentieth century, "many archeologists were optimistic that archeological discoveries had validated many of the historical claims of the Bible, if not the theological interpretations given to that history by biblical authors" (Laughlin 2000, 12). Much of the energy for historicizing the Bible radiated from Protestant literalist scholars beginning in the late eighteenth century. "The central absorbing interest" of much of archeology in the Holy Land, according to Laughlin, "is the understanding and exposition of the scriptures" (12). He adds that "many Israeli archeologist[s] still seem to operate from this perspective" (12), whereby secularization of the Bible is a national enterprise in Israel, carried out by hundreds of scholars, Jews and non-Jews, at all universities.

Biblical scholarship in historical Palestine has served to support a nationalist Zionist ideology that seeks to root itself in history by utilizing a text bearing a great deal of religious authority, even while its veracity is highly debatable. Israeli historian Benjamen Beit-Hallahmi (1992) writes: "Most Israelis today . . . regard the Bible as a source of reliable historical information of a secular political kind . . . The Zionist version of Jewish history accepts most biblical legends about the beginnings of Jewish history, minus divine intervention . . . The descent into Egypt and the Exodus era phases of a secular history of a developing people, as is the conquest of Canaan by Joshua. The Biblical order of events is accepted, but the interpretation is nationalist and secular" (119). Such entrenched beliefs flow directly into the Israeli political and military establishment and provide a central component of the indoctrination of citizens serving in its institutions. For example, the Israeli Defense Ministry has published a chronology of biblical events giving exact dates for the creation of the world (Masalha 2007, 26). According to their prophetic vision of history, Abraham is the first Zionist immigrant to Canaan (a parallel for Zionist immigration to Palestine beginning in the late nineteenth century), Joshua's conquest of Palestine and the killing and expulsion of the Canaanites maps onto the 1948 war, and King David's conquest of Jerusalem represents the 1967 Six-Day War through which Israel came to occupy the holy city and the rest of the West Bank.

Darwish's writings in the late 1980s and early 1990s comprise a new phase in his work as a poet-spokesman and cultural agent. He begins to investigate historiography and mythmaking, looking into the ways both are responsible for the occupation of his homeland, the disempowerment of his own people, and the people's alienation from their native landscape. His poetry delves into the politics of narrating history and sustaining myth in order to reveal the complexities and contingencies within that history. The poet argues that some central myths, taken as history and established as tradition, have helped justify Israel's relentless hostility toward the Palestinians and have delegitimized their claims to their historical homeland, ultimately estranging them from it. Yet as destabilizing for the Palestinians as Zionist mythology has been, the Israelis' own secularization of biblical myth into history provides ample evidence of the possibilities offered by diluting myth and transforming it into a modern force for the twentieth century. Such revised myths now exist on their own accord, and their authority rests as much on their separation from their biblical origins as on their association with them.

Darwish recognized how Zionist ideology, assisted by such mythmaking, has attempted to root European Jews in Palestine within a few generations. Myth for him became an area of contention and a potential means to retool the deep ideological structures of all those living in or belonging to Palestine. "The problem of Palestinian poetry," writes Darwish, "is that it set out without extra resources, without historians, without anthropologists; it therefore had to equip itself with all the necessary baggage needed to defend its right to exist" (1985, 82). Given that the Israelis have written their national myth and history using the Bible, a "narrative of birth that no one dreams of denying," how could the Palestinians "write a less mythic narrative" (82)?

Describing the quotidian life of Palestinians was meant to assert their organic belonging to the land. Still, demonstrating the historical existence of the Palestinians on their land by depicting their lives has proved less powerful than the geographical settings of mythical tales, when those myths are coupled with power (Darwish 1999b, 82). In other words, the real history of the land as belonging to the Palestinians does not withstand the assault of Zionist mythology. What the powerful believed mattered more than the facts. Hence, it was time for poets to enter this belief system, this mythical construct, to rewrite it and provide contentious alternatives to it. Poetry as an art form can evoke hymnal resonances associated with the practice of faith and can convey narratives with the authority of scripture and parable. Combining these two modes, Darwish began writing lyrical epics in this period.

In the poem "Al-hudhud" ("The Hoopoe"), Darwish mixes a variety of biblical and Quranic narratives to compose a myth (or perhaps a very large metaphor) of Palestinian existence and the state of suspension in which they find themselves. The poem combines the story of the biblical King Solomon (or Suleiman, considered a prophet in Islam), the story of Noah and the flood (narrated in the Bible and the Quran), and to a lesser extent, the Israelites' years of wandering in the Sinai Desert after the Exodus.

In the biblical version of the Sheba story, the Queen of Sheba journeys to Solomon carrying exotic gifts. She had heard of Solomon's wisdom and wanted to quiz him, and she eventually converts to his faith, having found him the wisest man that ever was. In the Quranic version, Solomon/Suleiman had at his command human armies, jinn, and animals, all of whose languages he spoke. Asking for the whereabouts of the hoopoe, Suleiman learns that the bird had been surveying the realm. The hoopoe tells him that he has discovered a sun-worshipping kingdom called Saba' (Sheba) ruled by a woman named Belqees. And so it is Suleiman that seeks Belqees in the Quran. She, threatened by his power and wishing to protect her people, decides to consider his offer and eventually converts to monotheism (referred to as "Islam" in the Quran). Solomon's Quranic hoopoe is not mentioned in the Bible.

In Darwish's treatment, the hoopoe replaces Noah's biblical dove that surveyed the land after the flood and informed him when to leave the ark. The Quranic version of Noah's story does not include a dove, and the hoopoe, which is detested and considered unclean in the Hebrew Bible, is considered an intelligent, dutiful believer in God. Darwish's mixing of the biblical and Quranic versions of the stories of Solomon and Noah is superimposed on the forty years of wandering in the desert that comprises a major chapter in Jewish mythology. Here is how "The Hoopoe" starts:

We haven't approached the land of our distant star. The
poem takes us

from the eye of our needle to weave for space a cape for
the new horizon to wear.
Captives, even if our wheat spikes leap over the fences
and swallows emerge
from the hold of our broken chains, captives of what we
love and what we want and what we are.

In us there is a hoopoe that dictates its letters to the
    distant olive trees of exile.
From our letters our alphabets returned to rewrite
what the rain inscribes in wild flowers on the distant
    stones.
And travel itself now travels, an echo from us and aimed
    at us. We were not to
return in spring to our small windows, and we were not
    leaves
for the wind to push on toward our coasts. Here and
    there a clearly defined line
for loss. For now, and for many years, we will hoist for
    sweet obscurity our dead as mirrors.
How many times will we lift the wounded to the small
    mountain to find the commandments?
Our message has re-emerged from our message. Here and
    there a clearly defined line
outlines the shade. How many seas will we cross in the
    desert? How many tablets will we forget?
How many prophets will we kill before our midday rest?
    And how many other people must we resemble to
    become
a tribe of our own? This road, our road is a grove of
    reeds on words ruffling
the edge of the cape between our homesickness and the
    land as it nears and dozes
in the saffron of our sunsets. Let's spread our will to raise
    our era to the time of the gods.
I am a hoopoe, said the guide to the master of creation. I
    am searching for a lost sky. (2005, 3:249–50)

The We speaking this poem are caught between stages of becoming: Solomon's people are waiting for Sheba's arrival—or,

alternately, Suleiman's army is waiting for a report from the hoopoe; Noah's followers on his ark are waiting for the signal to disembark; Moses's followers are wondering when their wandering will come to an end. They are in a state of captivity even as they continue to nurture themselves and others—"even if our wheat spikes leap over the fences."

Nonetheless, they seem to generate freedom for others through their captivity—"swallows emerge / from the hold of our broken chains." The speakers of the poem have created art that honors the lives of exiles like them. Their recollections are so palpable that their words have become a force of nature: "From our letters our alphabets returned to rewrite / what the rain inscribes in wild flowers on the distant stones." There's no journey in the world that finds them and does not carry their experiences with it—"travel itself now travels, an echo from us and aimed at us." They have paid their dues to have their "era" raised "to the time of the gods." Like the Israelites in Sinai, they have offered many sacrifices to the mountain to reach their own commandments and crossed "many a sea in the desert." Now they ask, "how many other people must we resemble to become a tribe of our own?"

The poem establishes the speakers' dilemma as they await an answer from their hoopoe, who comes and goes unpredictably, continuing his search. After he fails to "find the city in the city / and . . . a house of tenderness to spread over us the silk of calm" (2005, 3:251), he at last urges them to fly. They answer, "In our longings there's a great desire for flight, but people are birds that do not fly" (251). The hoopoe can only offer them a radical transformation, an inner flight toward transcendence:

He said, abandon your bodies to follow me and abandon
    this earth-mirage
to follow me. Abandon your names. Don't ask me for an
    answer.
The answer is the road, and there is no road that does not
    vanish in fog.
Fly higher than flying, higher than your sky so that you
    may fly
higher than the greatest love, higher than holiness,
higher than godliness, higher than feeling and free
    yourself
of the wing of the question of beginning and of destiny.
The universe is smaller than the wing of a butterfly
in the great courtyard of the heart. (257–58)

Darwish is closer to mystical and religious language here than
he has been in the past. The hoopoe advises his lost tribe to
"soar so that you may soar," to develop a uniqueness based
on their spiritual, intellectual, and emotional experiences—a
collective identity founded in attachment to the eternal.

But the physical world still aches and bears reminders of
what was lost, of the land they left that lies under "the flood":

How many times we've addressed the scent of a place
    saying, "Turn to
stone so that we may sleep." How many times
have we asked the trees of a place to strip themselves of
    the conquerors' adornments so that we may find a
    place of our own.
But "nowhere" is the place, and it has lodged itself deeply
    in the soul, away from its history.

Exile is this soul that distances us away from our land,
    asking us to be our beloved.
Exile is this land that distances us from our souls pushing
    toward strangers. (258–59)

The senses bring constant reminders of what was lost. Nature itself reminds the wanderers of their tragedy. It is interesting that Darwish here switches back and forth between his main portrait of a wandering people—a composite of Suleiman's, Noah's, and Moses's followers—to that of the Palestinians. Having structured the poem to incorporate more of the Palestinian experience, and having fitted their saga of loss into these biblical legends, Darwish can then switch the metaphor around. By the end of the poem, the tenor no longer needs to be contained within its vehicle to carry its meaning to the reader, and the Palestinians do not need an elaborate myth to tell their story.

It is precisely as this shift occurs and as more of the Palestinian experience is incorporated into the poem's mythical scaffolding that the protagonists in the poem take charge of their lives. When the hoopoe tells them that his "roads don't end at [your beloved's] door," they reply, "Our rituals will be complete / when we sail through this archipelago and release the captives from their tablets" (2005, 3:260). The speakers' mission for their own salvation will grow into the liberation of others. Through their long suffering, they have come to realize that the world is one, and that human experience is undivided.

As they explore this vision, they attest to the incompletion of any single Judeo-Christian-Islamic myth, and of the monotheist vision as a whole. Instead, their vision of a unified humanity is born out of devotion to the earth as a mother figure and granter of knowledge through her diverse offspring:

> On the earth there was once a spirit
> that the winds blew out and made destitute. Noah didn't
>   leave us all his divine knowledge
> and Christ walked away to Hebron . . .
> Here a body of apples is swimming in orbit. Water is its
>   waist belt
> as it traverses the eternity embedded in our praises, and
>   returns aiming for itself,
> a mother wrapping us in the conquest of her bared
>   tenderness, and hides what damage we'd done . . .
> Our mother is our mother.
> Mother of Athenians and ancient Persians, mother of
>   Plato, Zoroaster, Plotinus, mother of Sahrawardi,
> mother of all. (2005, 3:261–62)

The biblical, monotheist creeds are let go in favor of devotion to earth as mother, who nurtures and heals all and who supersedes them. This embrace of the earth becomes an embrace of human history and culture that is capable of dissolving differences among mother earth's most antagonistic children, all of whose accomplishments are celebrated.

As "The Hoopoe" continues, the bird as guide becomes less significant, and the speakers' appeals widen toward the forces of love, birth, and death. To the mother, the speakers say, "You nurtured us and fed us, mother, so that you'll feed our children as well. / But when will the weaning come?" (262). To love, whose "spider" has stung them, they say "have mercy on us" (263). But the speakers see a purpose through what loss and exile have given them: "Let this emptiness stretch to its delight, and let the human race complete through us its migrations" (254). Encapsulating their history, they see the power of their ongoing march and their ongoing journey:

> We have now learned that we came to return from an
> absence we had no wish for.
> And we have a life we have yet to try, and a salt whose
> eternity has not made us eternal.
> And we have steps no one has ever walked . . . (265)

Perhaps Darwish's other most innovative reinscription of biblical legend is his poem "Ḥajarun kanʿani fi al-baḥr al-mayit" ("A Canaanite Stone by the Dead Sea"), which plays off the story of the discovery of the Dead Sea Scrolls, as well as their content. The Dead Sea Scrolls were discovered in 1947 right as the Palestinian Nakba ensued after the state of Israel was established on historical Palestine. First discovered by a Palestinian shepherd in caves close to the Dead Sea, the scrolls were caught up in the conflict and had to be moved to Beirut for safekeeping. Darwish presents his Canaanite stone as a relic to be studied like the scrolls, presumably found near them and therefore just as valid. Like the Dead Sea Scrolls, his stone is meant to provide evidence of the considerable diversity of beliefs and practices in the Holy Land and affirms that "the origin" of Palestine is in "the multiplicity of cultural origins" (Darwish 1999b, 80). As a Canaanite relic, Darwish's poem/stone tablet stands as a testament to the natives whose existence on the land predated that of the invading Jews both in contemporary history and biblical myth. Made of stone, it is meant to last longer than the Dead Sea Scrolls made of parchment. The poem challenges the Hebrewfication of the history of Palestine undertaken by modern-day Israelis, and it emphasizes the multiple influences that have historically been brought to bear on the land and all its people.

The speaker in Darwish's poem is addressing a stranger, a hostile newcomer who stands for modern Zionists as well as for the biblical prophet Joshua. Darwish's underlying political assumption in the poem is that all that has taken place on the land of Palestine naturally belongs to the natives and to the descendants of the populations that have lived on the land (Yaḥyá 2003, 188). In the 1990s, Darwish urged Palestinians "to pragmatically distinguish between their historical homeland and a possible national state on the 'liberated' parts, and to differentiate between the geographical Palestine as a territory, and the political Palestine as a country" (al-Shaikh 2006).

This pragmatic acceptance of a political Palestine as only a part of the greater Palestine does not deny him or his fellow Palestinians the claim that they belong to the whole of the land. The Palestinians may give up their ownership of most of the land, but they will not give up their history on any of it. Darwish's poet-speaker is a resident native who has a sense of ownership of all of Canaan. He is an ancient and contemporary figure, "one of the salt shepherds at al-Aghwar" (the Jordan Valley Gorge), a reference to the shepherds who discovered the Dead Sea Scrolls. Darwish's shepherd extends

a hand of welcome to the armed visitor and invites him to
stay on:

> Stranger,
> rest your horse under our palm trees. On Syrian roads,
> foreigners exchange war helmets bristling with basil
> sown from doves that fly to the ground from the
>   housetops.
> And the sea died of boredom in the immortal testament.
>   Stranger,
> hang your weapon in our palm tree and let me plant my
>   wheat
> in Canaan's sacred soil. Take wine from my jars.
> Take a page from the book of my gods. Take a portion of
>   my meal,
> take the gazelle from the traps of our shepherds' song.
> Take the Canaanite woman's prayers at the feast of her
>   vines.
> Learn how we water our crops, how we build with stone.
>   Lay a single brick
> down and raise a tower for doves.
> Go ahead, be one of us, if that's your wish, neighbor to
>   our wheat.
> Stranger, take the stars of our alphabet
> and together we'll write heaven's message to man's fear
> of nature and man's fear of himself. Leave Jericho under
>   her palm tree
> but don't steal my dream, don't steal my woman's breast
>   milk
> or the ant's food stored in the cracks in the marble.
> Did you come to kill then inherit
> so that you add salt to the sea? (2005, 3:315–16)

Speaking to the stranger, who stands for Joshua and his invading armies after the sack of Jericho and for modern-day Israelis, the poet-speaker extends a rather broad hand of welcome. The stranger only brings arms to the land and is lacking in civility, failing to notice the exchange among soldiers of helmets brimming with basil. After instructing the stranger to put his weapon away, the shepherd offers him wine and a place to rest. He then offers to teach him to plant crops in this soil and to build a home out of the stones of the region. The gesture goes beyond material things, and the shepherd invites the potential neighbor to coauthor a new holy book with him.

As welcoming as the shepherd's message is, it also establishes the shepherd as the native whose traditions ought to be followed. Addressing his guest, the poet-speaker repeats the word *stranger* three times in the aforementioned passage, emphasizing his ownership and the guest's act of trespass. His welcome falls into the long-held traditions of hospitality still practiced in much of the Arab world today: "Houses are marked by a strong desire to receive visitors and, at the same time, to safeguard their own interiority, which is often described as *hurma* (sacredness or inviolability)" (Shryock 2004, 35). The poet-speaker immediately teaches the stranger what these inviolable possessions and places are—the shepherd's wife and his children and the share of other creatures in the bounty of the land. And though an invitation has been extended to the stranger to cowrite a book inspired by heaven to allay "man's fear / of nature and man's fear of man," the new communal philosophy ought not impinge on the individual's dream.

The aforementioned passage outlines, in mythic terms, a vision of natives and invading strangers (Palestinians and Israelis) in a single society where physical needs and shared labor and knowledge are the basis of harmony as they write a new life and myth together (Darwish 2005, 3:317). The shepherd cannot fathom any reason for the stranger's arrival other than to join his society and help shape it: "Did you come to kill then inherit / so that you add salt to the sea?" says the shepherd incredulously.

History, continues the shepherd, should teach the stranger that attempts at conquest are "futile." "You will not rise from history, and you cannot wash the sea's mist from your body" (317). The stranger does not realize that the place "has turned armies into wreckage and dust" and that all those who wished to erase the traces of the shepherd's ancestors were "enacting a farce from beginning to end" (317). Steering the poem toward the current Palestinian predicament, Darwish writes:

> No one
> conquers the sea. Cyrus, Pharaoh, Caesar, the Negus and others
> came to write their names with my hand on its tablets.
> So I wrote: The land is in my name and the name of the land
> is the gods who share my place on its seat of stone.
> I have not gone. I have not returned bearing elusive time.
> (318)

Like the contemporary Palestinians' assertion of nonabsence from the land even while in exile, the Canaanite shepherd declares his presence in real time. Again, Darwish contrasts imaginary time and historical claims with concrete experience. The shepherd senses eternity through habitual exchanges with nature and the elements, human practices that refuse to bow to invading armies and their dictates. Even when powerful invaders hold his hand to inscribe their names on the land, his hand disobeys them and instead affirms his name as belonging to the land and vice versa. Nor will self-reflexivity and isolation serve to grant the stranger a sense of autonomy or erase all traces of the native. "Of what use are mirrors to each other? My face is in your face," says the shepherd. In other translations, the latter part of the line reads, "we have a bond between us" (Darwish 2000a, 159). In either case, the stranger and the native, in blood and in text, have come into being under "the laws of crossbreeding" (Darwish 1999b, 83) and will continue to do so.

Darwish's project of inserting the contemporary Palestinian saga into myths of historical Palestine expands to include verifiable history in other poems during this period. In his references to the Crusades and to Mongol invasions of the region, Darwish finds a way to "observe the shadows of self and other, graspable in a more complex human journeying" (1999b, 81). In such long poems as "Hudna maʻa al-Maghul amama Ghabat al-Sindiyan" ("A Truce with the Mongols Near a Pine Forest") and "ʻAhda Ashara Kawkaban ʻala akhir al-Mashhad al-ʼAndulusi" ("Eleven Planets in the Last Andalusian Sky"), he begins to "inscribe the national on the universal, so that Palestine would not limit itself to Palestine" (1999b, 83). Homing in on the Muslims' expulsion from Andalusia, Darwish recognizes how Arab Spain has remained "a unique placeless space . . . a fleeting hetero-topia" (al-Shaikh 2006) upon which visions of heterogeneity can be projected and pursued.

Here Darwish also suggests that the Palestinian cause needs to absorb other experiences of displacements and set itself alongside them. Darwish's poem "Khitab al-Hindi al-Aḥmar ma qabala al-Akhir lil Rajull al-Abyaḍ" ("The Red Indian's Penultimate Speech to the White Man"), based on a text by Seattle, chief of Suquamish and Duwamish Native North American tribes, presents this desire to articulate a fellow subaltern's grief and to internalize his experience. In fact, much of "The Red Indian's Speech" proves to be a source for "A Canaanite Stone by the Dead Sea," and vice versa, suggesting that Palestinian identity can, and needs to, draw on heterogeneous sources, and that it is capable of providing a discursive anchor in the midst of past, present, and future exilic turmoil for all who experience such displacement.

Poetic Agency of the Deep Present and Deep Past

In the mid-1980s and early 1990s, considered by many to be Darwish's most ambitious period, we see his poems working on two temporal planes, or perhaps two different means of cinematic conveyance. The poems in *Lesser Roses* operate in the deep present; their imagery is that of a handheld camera. The point of view does not provide long shots, keeping us in medium range at most. The spatial and temporal presentation of the poems negates the potential for irony, as any perspective depends on what the people being viewed say or feel—in this case as they are trapped in airports or tight passages. Much also depends on the projection of these situations over appropriate metaphors and startling images. *Lesser Roses* provides the reader immersion in the strange mix of claustrophobia and utter displacement that Palestinians feel. Like Kanafani's protagonists in *Men in the Sun*, trapped inside the water tank of a tanker truck in the middle of a vast desert, they are in the flux of their dilemma and no sense of irony, historical or philosophical, can provide them solace.

In the longer myth-based and historical poems that appeared in *Ara ma Urid* (*I See What I Wish to See*, 1990) and *Aḥada-'ashara Kawkaban* (*Eleven Planets*, 1992), Darwish finds in history "a scene through which people, civilizations and cultures could circulate freely" (Darwish 1999b, 81). Emphasizing the ambiguity of history becomes an important tool to counter the single-minded Zionist vision of the past that claims historical certainty as the basis for its politics of exclusion. Darwish's rewriting of myth depends on fissures in national myths, and it focuses on past spaces of heterogeneity that have been erased. Expanding these spaces to include the present, as well as mythic and historical times, "Darwish's depictions of an expanded Palestinian identity and memory—which includes the Israeli Other as well as similar communities of the dispossessed—transgresses the paradigmatic boundaries of homogeneity in nationalism" (Celik 2008, 290). His rewriting of history and myth provides a reconciling rather than divisive narrative for Palestinians and Israelis. Expansive and inclusive in its past and future, Darwish's new mythology performs the requisite reenvisioning that needs to precede all difficult political arrangements. His calling as poet-visionary at this juncture is to prepare both the Israelis and the Palestinians for their necessary coexistence.

6

Who Am I without Exile?

*Anxieties of Renewal and a National
Late Style, 1995–2008*

In the summer of 2000, I visited the city of Ramallah to run a creative-writing workshop for young writers at the Khalil Sakakini Center. This center happened to house Darwish's office where he edited the journal *Al-Karmal*. I had very few chances to meet Darwish, and so I have little to personally report about him at that time. Rather, my revelation about the role of poetry in Palestinian culture came from the young poets I met and how they expressed their burgeoning poetic projects and ambitions, in which Darwish figured prominently, even as a shadow. The young poets' anxieties resembled those expressed by earlier groups of poets throughout the Arab world. Raised on Darwish's early and politically direct poems, new Arab poets since the 1970s have had to contend with Darwish's centrality (largely due to his being the uncontested poet of Palestine), which left them on the margins (see Bayḍūn 1999; Nasser 1999). Even as Darwish began to adopt new techniques and more subtle approaches, any poet who was perhaps gifted but who lacked Darwish's historical and cultural knowledge would have fared badly if he or she were to compete with or even try to compliment the great poet. This is all the more true for poets just starting out.

What remained for the young writers in Palestine, like the previous generation of poets in the Arab world, was the personal realm—an area that did not require vast cultural knowledge or any simplification to appeal to the masses. Given that the young poets were extremely skeptical of their national political structures and suspicious of the masses' need for perpetual uplift, their ventures into internal landscapes took on idiosyncratic forms. One of the poets I met in Ramallah was Anas al-'Aili, who was twenty-three. In 1989, at the age of twelve, al-'Aili was shot during the intifada as he and other boys threw stones at Israeli soldiers. He needed to be rushed to a hospital in Qalqilia, and it took an eight-hour operation to patch him up. I asked al-'Aili if he had written any poems about his injury or the intifada. He had not, he told me, partly because his heroism had become part of the uprising and partly because it was the street, the city, and its people that claimed his experience. He said it would take a great deal of effort for him to reclaim that incident from the collective memory, even as that memory keeps eroding in the same way that successive martyrs' names are overwritten by those of new martyrs on city walls. Furthermore, he did not want to be identified with that incident alone or with politics in any manner. In fact, he did not even want to be identified only with Palestine but rather seen as a person and poet outside all cultural and national frameworks.

Al-'Aili explores this search for self-sufficiency in "Plant," a poem in which the poet-speaker adopts the persona of a plant:

I am my home and my distance.
I inhabit my self
and die in it.
My roots are sails in the dirt
and my trunk the throne of the wind
and the creatures' resting place.
They throb into the earth
and I throb toward the sky.
I travel my branches.
I breathe the sun-filled horizon
and I knead water into birthless children.
I am my home and my distance.
I inhabit myself
and I die in it.
(*Ḍuyūf al-nār* 1999, 7)

Al-ʿAili's speaker manages to transcend human experience altogether and inhabit another form of life. Written as a dramatic monologue, the poem resounds with confidence as the plant describes its strengths and admirable qualities in terms a human being can understand. The plant's existence combines "home" and "distance," two opposing elements in our sense of space and mobility. The tree's roots and trunk hardly move, but they become necessary to other creatures that do— sails for ships, a seat for the ever-moving wind, and a nesting place for the scurrying creatures. When these creatures return to the earth, the tree "throbs" toward the sky. The tree's own body provides enough space for a journey, making it a contained universe, wide enough to breathe in the whole horizon. Its life promises to continue endlessly, since all it needs is some water to breed its "birthless children."

Al-'Aili's poem appears in *Ḍuyūf al-nār al-da'imūn: Shu'arā' min falasṭīn* (*Fire's Eternal Guests: Poets from Palestine*, 1999), an anthology of Palestinian poets under the age of thirty compiled by the Palestinian House of Poetry in Ramallah and published by one of the largest and most prestigious publishers in Beirut. *Ḍuyūf* includes no introduction, only a short postscript by Ghassan Zaqtan, a leading Palestinian poet and literary journalist a generation younger than Darwish. The other poems in *Ḍuyūf* are in a vein similar to al-'Aili's. The vast majority of them are in free verse, their tone varying from lofty to everyday speech, their content ranging from symbolist-inspired moods to quotidian deep imagery. None of the poems mention Palestine or Israel, nor do they address events or locations associated with the Israeli occupation or the Palestinian history of displacement, victimization, and struggle.

Zaqtan, aware of the stark presentation these poems make, states that the poems in *Ḍuyūf* "offer a new and different point of view of the Palestinian poetry scene" (1999, 163). He claims that this approach to poetry has been part of Palestinian literature all along and adds:

The centrality of the Palestinian cause has demanded that a text written in Palestine fall into the suggestions and references outlined by the politician's wish and conditions. And due to this perspective all writings that did not match this kind of reading and these conditions were repeatedly excluded. These marginalized writings began to pile up and grew outside our public media and platforms and began to penetrate unknown venues and explore obscure areas. Now it has come to pass that the margin (or writings from the margin) has become a majority, a wide connected belt that is approaching the center and is about to overwhelm it. It is to this growing margin that these poems belong. (1999, 163)

Zaqtan backtracks from this incisive though triumphant note when he adds that this new poetry "is not the whole of the Palestinian poetry scene per se" (163). Most important to Zaqtan is that these poems demonstrate Palestinian contribution to new developments in Arabic poetry, especially free verse (*qaṣidat al-nathr*). The poems demonstrate that Palestinian poets can exercise their full creativity despite their commitment to their national cause and the political demands placed on their individuality. The poets here are brought together because it is "their right to contribute to the Arab poetry of today to which they belong" (164). This new Palestinian poetry, adds Zaqtan, is "distinguished by a deep feeling for life and a highly selective approach toward language" which earns it "a place as a creative partner in the Arab cultural project" (164).

Zaqtan's statement recalls, ironically, Darwish's early years, when the young Darwish urged Arab critics not to consider him and the new poets of Palestine an extraordinary phenomenon but rather to see their poetry as part of the evolution of Arab verse. Yet whereas Darwish had urged that critics take him and his fellow poets to task and not lavish them with the "cruel love" (Darwish 1971, 23) of undeserved praise, Zaqtan finds himself in the opposite situation, trying to insert a new Palestinian poetry into the Arab consciousness in spite of the large place that Darwish occupies and to demonstrate that young Palestinian poets are as good as their Arab peers.

Most fascinating here is how *Ḍuyūf al-nār* asserts itself as an internal conversation among Palestinians and that this conversation is on display for all to see. Zaqtan's project of highlighting the young Palestinians' poetic accomplishments continues in the same track that Jayyusi followed in introducing her nation's literature to the world. "Palestinian poets are now among the foremost avant-garde poets of the Arab world," she writes (1977, 5). Like Jayyusi, Zaqtan wishes to demonstrate that Palestinians have not lost their capacity to make art or their general capacity for sensitive expression, compelling thought, and refinement, even after all these years of occupation, war, and banishment. In fact, they have become better artists in spite of them.

Zaqtan's description of this new burst of energy in Palestinian literature echoes Said's meditations on late style, in which he contemplates why and how an artist, late in life, discovers a new and perhaps radicalizing source of inspiration. In his posthumously published essay "Thoughts on Late Style," Said (2004) offers a succinct description of late style for which he drew on Adorno's (1984) analysis of Beethoven's last works. Said agrees with Adorno that Beethoven's late works represent a series of continuous ruptures that obfuscate time and closure, producing a sense of suspended agitation coupled with awe. Beethoven's late works, Said (2004) contends, "remain unco-opted by a higher synthesis" as "they do not fit any scheme, and they cannot be reconciled and resolved." Out of Adorno's (1984) reading of Beethoven, Said attempts to tease a paradigm for formal "lateness" that goes beyond the artist's sense of impending mortality and the desire to make a lasting mark on the world. In the veteran artist's work, Said recognizes a new energy and a new set of questions that realign the great composer's work, which can be as spontaneous and fresh as the emergence of a new, highly talented artist.

Said's interest in late style rests in the process of artistic creation, under extreme conditions and at seminal junctures, that forces the artist to disregard conventions (including his own) and unsettles his world despite the sense of purpose and identity it has given him. That this late style emerges in response to a sense of "lost totality"—and almost assuring that totality is undone—is relevant in the context of Palestinian poetry. Late style represents a condition in its own right: the unsettling effort toward a seemingly limited and immutable situation and even toward one's own history, having brought this situation into being and having grown adapted to it. Said (2004) sums up "the prerogative of late style" as an effort "to render disenchantment and pleasure without resolving the contradiction between them. What holds them in tension, as equal forces straining in opposite directions, is the artist's mature subjectivity, stripped of hubris and pomposity, unashamed either of its fallibility or of the modest assurance it has gained as a result of age and exile." Late style, as such, demands that one remain committed to one's vision without losing sight of the ghost of mortality or the concrete limits and opportunities within which individuals can affect the world around them, even as they face an obscure future.

Said's description here is extremely useful in discussing Darwish and the Palestinian cultural scene from the Oslo

Accord years of the 1990s onward. The variety in Darwish's last works and the self-interrogation that takes place in them demonstrate some of the energy and anxious determination that Said considers to be elements of late style. One can sense the same urgent desire for renewal within all facets of Palestinian society since the first Palestinian intifada began in 1987. By then, the Palestine Liberation Organization (PLO), the Palestinians' primary means of challenging Israel militarily, had lost on that front. Instead of impending mortality, the Palestinians have felt the force of impending deterritoriality as they witnessed their internationally designated homeland clawed away by settler colonial land grabs.

Palestinian artists sensed a failing in their approach to art and in the process of shaping and pronouncing their identity. Still, many Palestinians disagreed with the approach Darwish began to articulate in the late 1990s (see al-Shaikh 2006, 2009), which happened to coincide with Jayyusi's creation of a Palestinian canon. Critiquing her designation of Darwish as a special case in Palestinian letters, Salah Hassan contends that Jayyusi's assemblage of Palestinian literature in her anthology, which veered away from resistance literature and dismissed its future potential, "produced authoritative documents that surrender the radicalism of Palestinian liberation in favor of U.S. recognition" (Hassan 2003, 20; see also Ibrahim 2005). Nonetheless, the Palestinians' push since the Oslo Accords to renew their art and internal conversation is evident in the proliferation of Palestinian arts venues and associations, even during occupation, as well as in the continued increase of exhibits, publications, and performances by Palestinian artists throughout the world (see Laidi-Hanieh 2008). While receiving US recognition helped politically, what they needed was to see themselves "stripped of hubris and pomposity" in their own literature, now that the nation and its history had become a "mature" source for its individuals' "subjectivity" (Said 2004). For the young Palestinian poets in the *Ḍuyūf* anthology this meant they needed to explore spheres of time and space outside the Palestinian dilemma and its conventional vocabulary, and outside Darwish's sphere of influence. In so doing, they were operating within a larger national project characterized by elements of late style, in which Darwish, nonetheless, still figures prominently.

Toward a New Aesthetic Agency

From Identity to Identification

Earlier in this discussion, we saw that from various places of exile, Darwish provided powerful depictions of the Palestinian condition (deep present) and also took on history and myth (deep past) as fields of poetic action inclusive of various audiences, with an anticipated outcome that was discursive, conceptual, and by nature, long term. For another new start with a more radical approach, Darwish needed to reassess Palestinian literature and his role within it.

In the 1990s, looking back at his earlier works, Darwish states that his first efforts "lacked cultural understanding of the relationship between poetry and reality" (1999a, 22). The notion that it is the poet's job to defend or praise his people, and to be a ready commentator on important political events, even those that concern the people who matter most to him, is "an outdated concept of poetry," explained Darwish (23).

The kind of incitement and commentary on Palestinian life the poets had been offering had become mannered and cliché. Darwish began to argue that "the literature of provocation" is no longer "capable of surviving on its own through the next moment or epoch" (24). He doubted that "a whole literary tradition" could "stand on the inciting poem or the literature of direct struggle" (20). He writes: "We have about fifty terms that we must liberate ourselves from even if these words are necessary to express our historical moment and our psychological condition, but esthetically it's become necessary that we give them up because they've been so overused that it's become a joke that you can take these fifty words and write a poem out of them" (34). The literature of incitement, as Darwish terms it, covers only part of the Palestinian experience. As such, it could not contribute to the larger project of Palestinian modernization: "Modernization could not continuously remain tied to a liberation project once the individual is dealing with a natural and normal setting" (25). The "modernization" project Darwish posits in this 1999 interview assumes that Palestinians as a collective will live through more normative existential experiences that are not all the result of political contingencies.

In the past, according to Darwish, Palestinian literature was judged on the basis of these contingencies being imposed on its creation and by literary standards that arose from content addressing these conditions (Darwish 1999a, 24). As such, the national literature as a whole was an act of contingency tied to the collective cause, and its success was dependent on its contribution to that cause. In Darwish's view, this has not produced great art, and it is time to "begin to pay attention to the general rules and great ambitions of writing.

We should stop refusing to address Palestinian literature with normal literary critical skills and tools" (Yaḥyá 2003, 234). Darwish expressed these views during the Oslo Accord years and held on to them even as the second intifada ensued and the Palestinian/Israeli peace process came to a halt. Darwish's continued investment in the aesthetic component of cultural rejuvenation arises from his confidence in Palestinian national identity and culture. "I am one of those who firmly hold that the danger of physical, cultural and spiritual obliteration of the Palestinians has become remote," he argued (Darwish 2000b, 19). Feeling less threatened and with their survival somewhat secured, Palestinians no longer need "to praise [their] identity and to protect it . . . if you are safe, why would you praise yourself for being Palestinian?" (Darwish 1999a, 44). Darwish was already looking forward to the moment in 1998 when he would urge Palestinians to begin writing as if there were no occupation and to prepare themselves for their future (45). Palestinians had already begun this work, he argued, and had stopped waiting for a collective vision as an ideological guide: "Each one of us has started to look to his personal voice . . . We have ceased to wish to become heroes or victims" (Darwish 2000b, 22).

For Darwish, the end of heroism signifies a new awareness of recent political history that takes into account contemporary developments in literary and cultural criticism around the world. He states:

> The hero is tired of maneuvering between being a hero and a victim . . . He wants to become a normal human being. This transformation has taken place in numerous literary traditions . . . *Heroism has ended in modern literature*

... Now the marginalized is being glorified, *because history works differently now*, and because the poet is now aware that he is not a savior or rescuer, not a messiah or a prophet. (Darwish 1999a, 16; italics mine)

Darwish is perhaps speaking pragmatically and alluding to the Palestinian situation when he says that the hero has reached new challenges. In the eyes of the world, the Palestinian has moved from being "a refugee to being a freedom fighter to being a stone-throwing youth to finally a pragmatic political negotiator," explains Darwish (Darwish 1999b, 83). Heroism's end in Palestine coincides with both the end of the hero as an existential model in literature and with the end of grand, totalizing narratives around the world. For Darwish, the "normalization" of Palestinian literature is in keeping with contemporary global aesthetic standards and historical paradigms.

Besides this paradigmatic shift in the perception of the hero and the agency of the common man, Darwish also acknowledges that the Palestinians have lost to the Zionists in the struggle for control of their ancestral homeland. "We have been defeated," (Yaḥyá 2003, 235) he acknowledges, adding that "Palestine is defeated Troy" (Darwish 1999a, 23). This powerful parallel goes back to some of Darwish's earliest writings in the 1960s, in which Palestinian women sang, "We are the women of Troy . . . the conquerors receive what they wish / for they are strong . . ." (Darwish 2005, 1:162). The defeated need not despair, however, as they continue resistance through the candor and artistry of their cultural achievements: "We have been defeated, but should we throw away all our weapons. No! But language must

re-examine itself now and poetry too and should not contribute to distributing delusions. Poetry should try to raise
hope through an esthetic force and presence and not the force
of preaching, with the force of poetry not the force of the
message contained inside of it, which repeatedly says we're
victorious" (Yaḥyá 2003, 235). The weak and the losers
can write their history, too, adds Darwish, since "poetry is
an act of bias toward the victims and the weak" (Darwish
2000b, 19), especially contemporary poetry. The defeated
must, therefore, create their own myth to "resist the myths
of power and the powerful, and the songs of the victor that
erase him from history" (Darwish 1999a, 23). Defeat can
be turned into a source of energy, a way of confronting the
fact of one's existence. Such deep awareness can compel one
to keep working, striving, and expressing oneself: "I renew
myself by acknowledging defeat, and I resist through poetry
and language because this area is not defeatable" (Yaḥyá
2003, 235). When Darwish claims the aesthetic realm, or
poetry in particular, is undefeatable, it seems he is suggesting
that the arts provide an area closed to the contingencies of
politics. Focused on the senses, aesthetic endeavors appeal to
elemental responses to visual, aural, and other sensory stim-
uli, even as standards change with time. The lyrics of a song
may change with events, but our sense of who has a good
voice and who can play an instrument well goes beyond what
we think of the song's content. Similarly, in poetry, changing tastes have revolved around the basic musical, narrative,
linguistic pleasure to be expected from the art form. In that
sense, Darwish's positing of aesthetics as an independent
realm echoes the thinking of Immanuel Kant (2007) and
modernist, formalist theoreticians.

Works of art, according to Kant in *Critique of Judgment* (2007), are the willful acts of those who make them, but they are also wide open to interpretation by those who perceive them, since their makers may not have designated a purpose or rational need for their creations. And since the cause of a work of art precludes its effects, a piece of art, and the whole aesthetic realm by extension, cannot be engaged in relation to the circumstances or the social and material conditions in which it is produced (Kant 2007, 5). Works of art are therefore transcendental, since they do not rationally engage the material needs and conditions of their time and instead must be engaged without the context of history and location. Kant makes an effort to distinguish the "transcendental" analysis of aesthetic judgment from a study of the history or culture of taste. He defines the field of aesthetics as a domain in which particular feelings of pleasure and pain, independent of the laws of cognition and morality, are universal (82).

In Darwish's proposal, aesthetics as a transcendental force enlarging the imaginary and the sense of possibility provides a space that the repressive policies of the oppressor cannot enter. In fact, such spaces are created precisely because they are impenetrable, and aesthetic activity has rules to which the political and social do not apply: "We have our story as human beings . . . and we have our instincts, and this is the work of literature, and this is something that Israel has nothing to do with" (Darwish 1999a, 44). These areas that "Israel has nothing to do with" are "the eternal human questions that bear no direct relation to the occupation or liberation, nor the homeland or exile or the state or self-rule" (19). These areas, Darwish contends, can foster a

Palestinian space for expression and identity formation, and more importantly, preservation and exploration.

For Darwish, the aesthetic endeavor becomes a form of resistance to forces of occupation that wish to limit the Palestinian subject to his daily physical needs and concerns. To write literature that reiterates only this aspect of Palestinian life and to forbid the Palestinian writer from other explorations and sensations is to impose those limits on him:

> The occupation wishes to imprison the Palestinian poet in the cage of speaking about the occupation, and to keep him weeping about his symbolic mother, and keep him rotating around the first questions of existence . . . Do we have the right to cross the checkpoint, etc. *But for the person to exercise his full rights, if only in his imagination, or in his relation to his language, is an act of resistance to the conditions of occupation,* which has so far succeeded in cornering the Palestinian literary language into expressing the momentary and the present . . . and with unexceptional skill at that. (Darwish 1999a, 19; italics mine)

Darwish held on to these ideas even during the second intifada, which began in the fall of 2000 and resulted in a great deal of suffering for Palestinians and shattered hopes for peace with Israel: "Let's imagine that for fifty years, a people have written nothing except the occupation or that it is an occupied people, and about the compulsion to fight the occupation. But what is amazing and miraculous is for us to write something else, for me to write my humanity in the middle of darkness and siege. For us to continue to write what the occupation dictates to us is an expected reaction for which the occupier is ready to respond, it is a surrender of language" (20). Darwish added that Palestinians should undertake this enterprise everywhere, for "it seems that our real and imaginary deliverance is a cultural one" (Darwish 2000b, 23). The movement of Palestinian culture in various open spheres, languages, and media "delivers it from the pressure of the enclosed political present" (22–23). But Darwish does not want these external factors to completely disappear. The Palestinian work of art has to win its admirers throughout the world on the basis of its engagement with aesthetic concerns and universal questions. In the work of art, formal pleasures seduce the viewer to identify with the artist's own unconscious fantasies, which then transmit various pleasures and sensations associated with the artist to the viewer or reader (Segal 1998, 215). For psychoanalyst Hanna Segal, the aesthetic pleasure proper—that is, the unique kind of pleasure derived from a work of art—is due to this process of identification. "Aesthetic pleasure arises due to an identification of ourselves with the work of art as a whole and with the whole internal world of the artist as represented by his work" (215). In other words, every aesthetic pleasure has to do with reliving the artist's experience of creation. Darwish's call for the aesthetic intensification of his and other Palestinians' art stems from a desire to enhance the possibilities for identification with their works.

Earlier works of Palestinian art, including his own, helped shape Palestinian identity by reflecting common experiences that Palestinians recognized as clearly and undeniably their own. But in Darwish's opinion, such works lay fallow, incapable of generating identification even among Palestinians. The questions Palestinian art addressed had to arise from personal points of view and personal experiences, to which unexpected perspectives and the rules of artistry, pleasure, and affectation apply. Only through a deep engagement with aesthetics, through which readers and perceivers are artistically transported and seduced by the recreation of their experiences, can Palestinian artists truly generate identification with their concerns.

Darwish argues that he does not advocate that Palestinians "transcend their reality," only that "we write our story better" (Yaḥyá 2003, 235), with greater attention to form and technique. The Palestinian component need not appear directly or at all. What is important or "amazing and miraculous is to write my humanity in the middle of darkness and siege" (Darwish 1999a, 21). The Palestinian artist should therefore seek first and foremost to cause what Victor Shklovsky (1988) called "special perception" (25) of his work of art, so the reader can create "a vision of the object" (25) from which she or he can draw meaning. Once the reader or viewer has come to share an experience and to generate his or her own experience through a work of art, he or she comes to identify with the artist who provided this human connection. Upon realizing that the artist is a Palestinian, the reader or viewer can then *reperceive* the work's importance, given its "amazing and miraculous" inception.

As he adopts a Kantian definition of aesthetics for a formalist rather than functional approach to the creation and perception of art, Darwish also incorporates criticisms of this outlook, stressing that one cannot hope to understand art without comprehending the economic and political circumstances in which it was created. As such, even as we are asked to read a Palestinian poem guided "first and foremost by elements intrinsic to the poetic art itself" (Zaqtan 1999, 237), we are also invited to read such a poem as an assumption of agency, since it is created as a response to a given socioeconomic and political setting.

Al-ʿAili's poem "Plant" will assist here to further probe this point. Earlier we read the poem with a dislocated, formal approach and saw how the poem itself is an attempt to transcend location and circumstance. In that manner, it provides a metaphor that can illuminate human longing, especially when mobility and growth seem irreconcilable. When placed again within a Palestinian context, the poem begins to offer other readings and can be seen as an attempt to make the best out of the poet-speaker's immobility. Even during the relatively calm 1990s, during which the poem was written, most young men like al-ʿAili, especially those with a record of confronting the Israeli army, were liable for arrest and detention. The poet states, "I am my home and my distance" (*Ḍuyūf* 1999, 7) not simply to celebrate autonomy, but also to tell us that he is stationary, like a tree. Only through the use of metaphor can he sail away and fly with the wind, and only by celebrating his immobility can he overcome the need for such freedom. Adopting the persona of a tree is a way of overcoming the forces that have obliged the poet to stay put against his will. We had read the poem as a celebration of the ability to nurture an inner life by internalizing the life processes of other creatures, but knowing that the poet is a Palestinian transforms the poem into a statement of psychological resistance. The Palestinian presence becomes a salient critical subtext that can be brought into it by the outsider/reader if he or she wishes, and can enrich her or his perception. But before the reader can celebrate the poem's miraculous making, the work of art itself has to succeed on aesthetic terms—on its form and technique rather than its context.

The Travails of Separation of Poet and Nation-State

In 2000, Darwish published a book-length lyric poem titled *Jidariya* (*Mural*) to wide acclaim in the Arab world. A few years before, perhaps while writing *Sareer al-Ghariba* (*The Stranger's Bed*), Darwish had told a documentary filmmaker that he wished for the Palestinian trauma to end, just so that he would know how good a poet he is (Bitton 1997). The poet was still suspicious that his work, attached as it was to Palestine and the Palestinians, could only be judged on the basis of that attachment. The shadow of "the content" obscured and marginalized the hard work of his poetic artistry (see Darwish 1971, 1979; Wāzin 2006). He longed for an opportunity to demonstrate his skills in the daylight of artistic judgment alone. With *Mural*, Darwish appeared to do that, and he received the acclaim he needed. For the acclaimed Bahraini poet Qassim Haddad, *Mural* was the first time he was able to "read Darwish without his Palestinianness and I must say that that feeling pleased me" (Haddad 2009). Such a sentiment would have pleased Darwish, too. Written in France shortly after he survived major heart surgery, during which he was briefly in a coma and had a near-death experience (Wāzin 2006, 46), *Mural* celebrates the poet's survival and his new lease on life and poetry.

Darwish's poet-speaker here is exhilarated by oblivion:

Nothing ails me at the gate of Judgment day,
not time or emotions.
I feel neither the lightness of things
nor the heaviness of premonitions . . .
There is no nothingness here

in the no-here, in the no-time,
of no existence.
(Darwish 2006, 442–43)

The world is white in "this sky of the absolute" (443). The
speaker suspects he has died previously because he "know[s]
this vision" (443) and knows he is heading somewhere he
does not know. From this nexus of oblivion and erasure
emerges renewal and possibility, and the clean slate is the
poet himself, achieving the state he had told the aforementioned filmmaker he wished he could achieve:

> Maybe
> I am still alive somewhere and I know
> what I want to be . . .
> One day I will be what I wish to be,
> one day I will be an idea, carried by a sword
> to free a wasteland with a book in hand,
> as if it were rain falling on a mountain aching,
> aching with the grass bursting through its soil,
> somewhere where power had not won
> nor where justice has become a fugitive.
> One day I will be what I wish to be . . .
> one day I will be a poet . . .
> I am the message and the messenger.
> I am the tiny addresses and I am the mail.
> One day I will be what I wish to be. (446–47)

Darwish's repetition of "One day I will be what I wish to
be" vacillates between chant and plaint; the hope it seeks is
singed by a long struggle with despair. Most inspiring, and
also humbling, to the young poets I worked with in Ramallah

was Darwish's declaration that he wishes to be a poet one day. What horizons, aesthetic or otherwise, could this poet be seeking if he thinks he has never been a poet to begin with?

Implied in the sketch of the new poet Darwish would be is the whiteness (of death) that he wished to fill (in defiance) with his poetry, the whiteness of the blank page (the pages he filled with poetry erased and forgotten), and the whiteness of the identity card on which his fate had been inscribed. All the poet needed to do in this new space/place, as the nurse instructed him, was to "remember your name to keep it safe. / Do not betray it, / pay no mind to the banners of the tribes. / Be a good friend to your name" (Darwish 2006, 447). Darwish went on to recite this poem to thousands of listeners and television viewers, aware that the audiences had come to hear him because of Palestine, but they stayed attentive because of the poetry, which was rhythmic, engaging, and pleasurable, and had little to do with Palestine.

After years of displacement, what happens to the Palestinian poet as stand-in for the national subject when these national pressures ease? Even before *Mural*, Darwish knew there was another side to the luminous world discovered upon defeating death, a side that repeatedly tells the poet that because he has been an exile for so long, he cannot in fact be what he always wished. In *Sareer al-Ghariba (The Stranger's Bed*, 1996) we find Darwish's poet-speaker alone, outside the borders and national mood of Palestine, and at a loss as to what to do with his freedom:

> Who will tell me now,
> "Forget your yesterday, and dream with
> the whole of your free subconscious mind"?

My freedom sits near me, with me, on my knee
like a house cat. She stares at me and all that you'd left
behind last night. Your lilac shawl,
videotapes about dancing with wolves, a necklace
of jasmine grown on the moss of the heart.
What will my freedom make of itself, after your night,
the night of your last winter? . . .
My freedom and I sat silent staring at our night.
Who am I? Who am I after the night of your last winter?
(574–76)

The poet and his freedom have become docile and domesticated like a cat. His beloved had urged him to forget his yesterday and engage his imagination. Unlike other poems in *The Stranger's Bed*, in which the poet cannot stop himself from alluding to his beloved in mythical and historical terms, here we find him conscious of the need to let go of the past but unable to do so. The poem itself is titled "A Cloud from Sodom," as if to emphasize this inability. In other parts of the poem, the more recent past—like that which haunts a shell-shocked soldier—also exerts its presence. The speaker notes how the street is now empty, how no shadow followed him, and how, unlike the days of "Identity Card" or even "Athens Airport," there is no "guardsman to ask me, 'What is your name?'" (576)

And just as the female beloved commands the speaker, "'Forget your yesterday, and dream with / the whole of your free subconscious mind,'" trying to steer him toward a new source of inspiration, the poet is also forced to confront the emotional and conceptual paradigms that have oriented his life and artistry. Another female speaker in *The Stranger's*

Bed (this time Ulysses's wife, Penelope), tells him "I am not a land / or a journey. / I am a woman, no less and no more" (Darwish 2005, 599). Darwish's female interlocutors in *The Stranger's Bed* understand that there is no conflict between the imagination and the body, and they are aware that things need not be transformed into myth or abstraction to reveal their "essence." But Darwish's male poet-speaker is deeply attached to placing the real into the legendary—he needed to, culturally and politically. He is not comfortable with the mind free from a guiding mission or a threatening force.

This estrangement from the self and from the beloved is what Darwish's speaker repeatedly fails to escape. It becomes the mindset into which he retreats, because it has been his most comfortable existential mode—a cycle of perpetual departures and separations, best expressed in the poem "Who Am I Without Exile?":

> A stranger by the riverbank,
> and like a river, water ties me to your name.
> Nothing returns me from my distance
> to my date palm, not peace or war.
> Nothing can insert me in the scriptures. Nothing,
> nothing, shines from the high tide or low,
> swaying between the Euphrates and the Nile.
> Nothing can force me to disembark
> from the Pharaoh's ships. Nothing carries me
> or places a thought on my shoulder.
> Not longing or a promise.
> What shall I do?
> What shall I do without exile
> on this long night
> of staring at the water? . . .

Nothing can make me leave
the butterflies of my dream
to face my reality, not dust or fire . . .

We have become weightless like our houses
in the distant winds . . .

We have been released
from the gravity of the land of our identity.
What shall we do?
What shall we do without exile,
and this long night of staring at the water?

Nothing of me remains except you,
nothing of you remains except me,
a stranger caressing his beloved stranger's thighs.
Woman, stranger, what shall we do
with all the quiet that surrounds us?

What shall we do without exile? (648–51)

The word *nothing* erases what comes before it and leaves the
heavy traces of itself everywhere in the poem. Return from
long absence is impossible even if, in the case of Darwish, the
return is physically possible. Exile has sown memories in the
mind, rooted and reared like trees until they become separate
creations, bearing all the traces of the past and surpassing it
in beauty, and therefore impossible to replant in the soil of
reality. Here again in *The Stranger's Bed* the poet-speaker
attempts to insert himself in myth in order to bear, and even
embrace, reality as it fails him. His return is not the Exodus
and cannot be likened to anything foretold in the scriptures

and myth. Nostalgia fails to make the return attractive, and the promise of a better future also fails. Without the gravity of the land of his identity, the speaker and his beloved have become weightless, like the tents that sheltered his people upon their fearful escape from home in 1948. Love itself fails to overcome the sense of nothingness. The two lovers have subsumed each other; their presence is marked only by what they see of themselves in each other. The crisis, therefore, is not that lovers cannot join to make each other whole, but that the sense of nothingness persists.

In exile, however, the binaries that the poet and his beloved had placed opposing each other are set precisely so as not to cancel one another out. In exile, the poet can keep his "distance" and his "date palm," his "nostalgia" and the "promise" of the future, his departures and landings, his Nile and Euphrates; traversing among them, he can become the tide swaying between. Exile, despite all the pain associated with it, gave the poet an inflated appreciation of his capacity to contain division. The poem's repetition of "staring at the water" points to this narcissism; longing is directed inward, and all forms of identification with the other reflect only the self ("nothing of you is left except me"). But now—or perhaps it had always been so, we are not sure—this gazing at oneself takes place in the dark ("this long night of staring at the water"). The old narcissistic pleasure of self-reflection is failing the poet, and contemplating his actions, he repeatedly receives nothing.

Darwish's portrayal of this scene by the river does not merely suggest the melancholy of his speaker and the reader, but resounds with dread. Earlier in this same volume, there are two references to Paul Celan, the great poet and Holocaust survivor, who committed suicide perhaps because he "realized that once you have penetrated the kingdom of night you have reached the end" (Wiesel 1990, 8). Celan killed himself by leaping into the freezing Seine, the same river by whose banks Darwish wrote most of *The Stranger's Bed*. For Darwish, the largesse of exile has been aligned with the grandeur of his and his people's vision of Palestine. As early as 1984, he anticipated a future disillusionment in the utopian vision of their lost homeland he and his countrymen had built and predicted disappointment in his return to it, as unlikely as that seemed at the time:

> How wide the revolution,
> how narrow the journey!
> How grand the thought,
> how small the nation! (Darwish 2005, 2:411)

The dream of Palestine reared in exile had become a mode of existence, difficult but familiar. Allowing one to defer arrival and settlement perpetually, exile detains the poet in the self he knows best, but it also keeps the stranger estranged, even in the homeland, even as he lies in his beloved's bed.

7

Parting Words

The Poet Appropriates Contingency

The beginning of the second intifada in 2000, combined with
the collapse of the peace process, especially the return of full
Israeli military occupation of the West Bank and the sieges
imposed on the major Palestinian cities, brought a new era of
Palestinian history that one would expect to have intruded
on Darwish's private existential investigations. The mind that
had been meditating on the white slates of death and on oblivion and the dark seas of life beyond the familiar waterways of
exile would now have to address the grays and khakis of military convoys and the red of firepower and blood. Darwish's
response to the second intifada was, in fact, to protect the
project he had begun with *The Stranger's Bed*, to shield the
impenetrable spaces he had encouraged all Palestinian writers to create for themselves. He did not lapse, as he did in Beirut, "by becoming one with his reader" (Darwish 1999a, 33);
rather, he sought a way to stop the "relative" circumstances
from encroaching on his conceptual investigations.

Retaining his focus on his art did not mean that he
stopped responding in poetry to the events of the second intifada, however; he did so almost right away, and continued

to do so with a tactful sense of timing and in an immediate, but collected tone. One of Darwish's most read poems at the time of its publication was an elegy to Muhammad al-Durra, a ten-year-old Palestinian boy whose death by Israeli fire was televised and broadcast around the world in the fall of 2000, a few days after the al-Aqsa intifada ignited. For Darwish, writing about such an incident seemed inevitable, "an expression of the organic connection between poetic language and the reality it confronts and the world from which it comes" (Yaḥyá 2003, 204). Failure to respond would uproot the poet from spontaneous interaction with the world, a faculty that could not be allowed to grow dull. But Darwish states that he had begun to approach writing this kind of occasional poem differently: "I tried in the Muhammad al-Durra poem to write what would be an objective poem, empty of oratory riches or ornate allusions, a poem that depicts and does not scream" (Yaḥyá 2003, 204).

The challenge to poetry on an occasion such as the death of a child, televised to millions of viewers, was that "language could not match the level of shock" (Yaḥyá 2003, 204) rendered by the camera. "Poetry had to become a second, hidden camera, so that it can quietly create the needed effect. Poetry must attempt to have its whispers heard because its screams and shouts could never be heard in the midst of the loudness of violence" (204). The poem, by snatching the event out of the silence-inducing hegemony of the electronic image, can then contribute to the creation of meaning through a quieter retelling that provides the needed catharsis of elegy.

Darwish published another poem shortly afterward that became an event itself. "Al-Qurban" ("Blood Offering") was written as Palestinian militant groups began to use suicide bombers in response to the Israeli reoccupation of Palestinian territories. The poem is an address to the martyr by the leaders of his society, who sent him to become a martyr on their behalf. Darwish recognizes the essential ambivalence of "the priests" who offer the martyr as "scapegoat" to the gods and to eternity in order to achieve success on earth. They have no access to heaven but the martyr, and no other way to free their society or purify it. They ask the martyr who was "born out of fire and light" to "go alone, alone" and to proceed quietly toward paradise. "Blood Offering" threw Darwish into the fray of a heated debate between Palestinians who felt the need to fight back by any means necessary and those who saw the use of suicide bombers as unethical and counterproductive to the national cause.

A few years later, Darwish published another timely poem, "Anta munḏu al-'ana ghairak" ("You, from now on, are not yourself"). With it, he addressed the strife in Gaza between Palestinian forces loyal to the democratically elected Hamas and those of the PLO-dominated Palestinian Authority, which led to expulsion of the latter from the area.

> You from now are not yourself.
> Did we have to fall from such a high place, did we have
>   to see our blood on our own hands, to realize that we
>   are not angels?
> Did we have to reveal our immodesty to the world so that
>   our truth no longer remains chaste?
> O how we lied when we said we are an exception!
> (Darwish 2007b)

Unlike earlier works, such as those written during the bombardment of Beirut in 1982, in which the urgency of the situation had its own generative and animated vigor, here Darwish's pace is slow and deliberate, issuing a judgment against the Palestinian subject and collective with the sobriety of deep disappointment and grievance. Most devastatingly, the poem admonishes by stating, "you are not who you had said, and believed, yourself to be" (Darwish 2007b). The poet becomes the nation's confessor and priest, taking his people to the depths of their despair to show them just how far they have fallen. The poem is painful, and its effect undeniably cathartic.

Though they were emailed and texted to and from hundreds of thousands of readers and were reprinted in tens of Arabic publications, none of these powerful, timely, highly popular poems appeared in Darwish's recent books. When asked about the elegy "Muhammad al-Durra" and the poem "Blood Offering," Darwish stated that he would not "spend a great deal of effort in defending their esthetic qualities" (Yahyá 2003, 205), hence their exclusion from his books. Having written such poems, Darwish recognizes poetry's ability to influence its historical moment, if only in the short term. In the case of the al-Durra elegy, which is probably the most conventional of the poems discussed in this chapter, poetry can help sustain a beleaguered population by articulating its grief. And in the cases of "Blood Offering" and "You, from now on, are not yourself," the poet engages contingencies deeply aided by music, metaphor, and allusion, and his poetry provides an important, broad, and perhaps revolutionary critique with immediate consequences.

Despite its immersion in the moment and the fact that it was wielded as a political gesture, the poem here cedes its claim on posterity. Such occasional poems do not rise to the highest aesthetic level, according to Darwish's discourse as outlined earlier, because they refuse to engage the experience they address beyond its context. Written out of emotion and justifiable only in the moment, these poems are meant to affect change immediately; the emotion that produced them could not reasonably be sustained beyond the crisis they address. They will not on their own be viable works of art, among the poet's aesthetically successful poems.

The short shelf life that Darwish has assigned poems like "Blood Offering" in which he critiques his society's failings also suggests that he believes these failings are correctable and do not constitute a flaw in the character or shape of the nation. It also suggests that the poet's passionate grief or enraged anger at his nation is only temporary. The poet has the right to scold briefly but not to condemn for eternity; he has the right to weep for a victim but not to turn his poetry into funereal sentimentality.

Darwish's dual approach to poetic composition (with some poems meant to expire) suggests an understanding of temporality as an ingredient in poetic agency, and a facet of the poet's authority. To begin with, the poet should not rely on events to guide the intervention of his agency but rather on his poetry as poetry. He cannot afford to rely on continuous political change as a source for poetic vision, in the same way that he cannot afford to write according to the dictates of his audience. The poet earns authority through the works that endure beyond their context and that continue to provide a renewable philosophical, existential, and political outlook for his reader. Consequently, it is this ability to endure that grants the poet authority to speak on immediate contingencies. Interventions in contemporaneous discourse have the weight of the poet's achievements behind them and are seen as necessary detours from the poet's usual focus on larger abiding subjects and concerns. Such interventions, in Darwish's approach, need not become part of the poet's recognized corpus but must pass on as exceptional direct engagements in the nation's immediate affairs.

It is therefore interesting to look at Darwish's book-length poem *State of Siege* (2002), given the poet's focus in his late period on "absolute" rather than "relative" concerns. *State of Siege* was written in the second year of the al-Aqsa intifada (2000–2005), during which the Israeli army reimposed military rule on the West Bank, placing several Palestinian cities under siege and placing a severe blockade on Gaza. Darwish's justification for writing such a responsive book perhaps falls within his belief that Palestinians must retain some "'defensive nationalism' that would preserve their collective memory" (al-Shaikh 2009, 201), especially as they remain "a country on the verge of dawn" (Darwish 2006, 178), their statehood perpetually deferred. Darwish's concept of defensive nationalism alludes to the beginning of Palestinian nationalist struggles in the 1960s, when diverse groups with contending political ideologies were forming the founding institutions of the Palestinian liberation movement (Farsoun and Aruri 2006, 190–200). In articulating the Palestinian national charter in 1968, the then-strong leftist current stressed that Palestinian nationalism "transcend chauvinistic nationalism so that

Palestinians do not produce a replica of the Zionist dream" (al-Shaikh 2009), but instead present a vision of an alternative multisectarian, multinational state with a secular, progressive government geographically comprising the whole of historical Palestine. In Darwish's view, a sense of nationalism was needed then, as well as now, for the Palestinians to sustain the structures necessary to unite the population and hold on to their territory when both are at risk.

Darwish's sketchy notion of defensive nationalism resembles what Spivak (1999, 4) called "strategic essentialism," a political stance taken by subaltern groups that involves the strategic use of positivist essentialism in a scrupulous manner to achieve political ends. The subalterns temporarily essentialize themselves and bring forward their group identity in a simplified way while debating issues related to group diversity and identity. In Darwish's defensive nationalism, the "temporary" use of strategic essentialization becomes "defensive," by which we understand a sense of minimalism, and whereby defensive nationalism becomes "minimal nationalism" (Darwish 1999a, 44).

In their stateless situation, Palestinian writers and artists thus have a role in "protecting the essence" (Darwish 1999a, 44) of a culture by providing conscientious responses to the suffering of the people around them and to whom they belong. Palestinian writers, like the rest of their fellow citizens, cannot avoid this suffering and cannot avoid being impacted by politics and participating in it in some level, contends Darwish (Darwish 2000b, 15). Engaged as they are in creating impenetrable individual spaces, Palestinian artists must continue to respond to the suffering around them lest they fall into solipsism and nihilism (Yaḥyá 2003, 213).

State of Siege arises from this protective impulse. Darwish subtitles the poetic sequence with the statement "This text was written in January 2002 in Ramallah," thus emphasizing the time and conditions under which the writing occurred. We note also that the poet calls his work a "text" and not a poem, and we are invited to see it as a journal of sorts. These cautionary gestures are reminiscent of the poet's subtitling of his *Madiḥ al- ḍul al-ʻali* (*Praise of the High Shadow*, 1983) as a documentary poem. *State of Siege* is a poetic text nonetheless, since it is broken into lines of verse, mostly metered, a great many of which are in rhyme. Yet whereas *Praise of the High Shadow* launches into an incantatory mode from the very beginning, *State of Siege* is episodic and meditative. Having decided to make a book out of his immediate response to being under siege, Darwish appears to be testing his own waters by proposing a work of art to us (according to his definition and practice) while also demonstrating a degree of caution about the work's artistry. He had argued that writing about immediate circumstances cages the Palestinian artist in the prison the occupier built. The challenge for Darwish in *State of Siege* is to take on this "relative" situation and find the absolute and cosmic elements in it.

Cautious or not, Darwish assumes the role of a collective spokesperson with a great deal of ease:

> Here on these low slung hills, facing the sunset,
> here within time's shot range
> near gardens of severed shadows
> we do what prisoners do,
> we do what the unemployed do—
> we nurture hope. (2006, 177)

Darwish's use of the first-person plural is emphatic and unencumbered, as if he had not cried out in *Mural* that he has yet to become who he wants to be, or as if he has not cried repeatedly at the conclusion of the poem, "I am not for myself, I am not for me" (2006, 537). The steadiness and collected tone in *State of Siege* suggest that the poet is indeed who he is; that speaking in We is a conscious, calculated decision; and that such a responsibility has not been imposed upon him by others. Perhaps it is the force of habit, or the poet's aforementioned confidence that the annihilation of Palestinian culture has become impossible.

The sense of confidence in Darwish's ability to deliver his poetic effect without raising his voice or demarcating his musical skills is also reflected in his prosodic choices. The structure of *State of Siege*, made up of 115 generally short stanzas that vary in length and subject matter, allows the poet to shift his focus in unpredictable ways, throwing poetic unity to the wind and favoring a postmodern sense of closure, the parts creating a tenuous whole. These formal choices make *State of Siege* a spontaneous as well as heavy-handed text. While the poet is free to say what he wants in whatever way he wishes, he also demonstrates a great deal of control over the poem with short, almost aphoristic stanzas. He avoids mere venting and neutral description, instead focusing on squeezing insight and wisdom out of his condition. Eschewing a sequential arc, the poet offers us a view of the state of siege and its implications in multiple, collage-like pieces, as if we are walking through a site of devastation, deciding what remains and what has been lost.

Continuing in Darwish's revamped (late) style, *State of Siege* is also a retrospective look at the poet's corpus. We encounter in this poem images from his early work, such as the grieving mother and the adversary's soldiers, who seek understanding and sympathy from the occupied they murder; we read about the martyrs who led the struggle and hear the poet-speaker lament his imprisonment, and that of his people, in time and place; biblical and mythical figures such as Job and Achilles make an appearance, as well as the poet's beloved stranger and her bed.

State of Siege, while providing a means to comprehend the poet and his people's perennial Trojan crisis, also provides the poet an opportunity to critique his own work and his previous approaches to poetic agency. Darwish is the supplicant before the confessor, the besieged before the befuddled besieger, the champion of lyric and quotidian time standing over the corpse of epic heroism.

Of specific interest here is Darwish's self-interrogation on these issues and on the motifs and strategies with which he shaped the Palestinian subject and culture. The poet takes on the fertility motifs he presented in his early work, especially the metaphor of the martyred bridegroom wed to the feminized land. In a remarkable passage, the poet presents a mother seeking her lost son. She is told that her son has just gotten married, a euphemism for his martyrdom. After the wedding celebration, she asks after the whereabouts of the newlyweds and is told they are "there above the sky, two angels / consummating their marriage" (2002, 214).

> So I sang out my ululations
> and danced and sang and danced until I fell down
> with a stroke. And so dying I asked,
> "O my beloveds, when will this honeymoon end?" (214)

In this short passage, Darwish undermines a paradigm he had championed for years, and to which his countrymen still adhered by holding wedding ceremonies at the funerals of martyrs. Having gone along with the celebration, the grieving mother wonders how long this fiction will go on, how long her people will continue to delude her. Celebrating martyrdom and pairing fertility with death have been an unsatisfactory response to personal loss, an unsatisfactory solution to collective trauma, because they require the perpetuation of an unverifiable redemption.

Later in *State of Siege*, the icon of the martyr that the poet celebrated in earlier work confronts him directly. "Where were you?" the martyr asks the poet. He then commands the poet to erase the praise he has heaped on the martyrs:

Toss back into the dictionaries all the words
you gave to me as gifts.
And be gentle on the sleepers and lower the drone of your
echoes. (Darwish 2002, 245)

The martyr goes on to "besiege" the poet several more times, telling him that he never wished for the virgins of paradise and that he loved his earthly freedom most. Finally, the martyr tells the poet not to walk in his funeral procession, for he only wanted those who knew him to do so. "I need no one's cordiality" (248), he tells the poet.

The distrust that the martyr expresses of the poet's earlier declamations, and of poetry in general, occupies a central place in Darwish's discourse in *State of Siege*. The poet, addressing poetry and mocking his verse, states, "To poetry, besiege your siege" (2002, 225), quoting the words he used in his highly enthusiastic, combative earlier poetry in "Aḥmad al-Za'tar" and *Praise of the High Shadow*. With evident self-mockery, the poet commands poetry to end its siege and to release its grip on his imagination, perhaps by lowering "the drone of [its] echoes" (245). The poet later cautions the reader, "don't trust the poem" (251), suggesting the reader should be skeptical of the poet's authority. Pursuits and claims of heroism are also not to be trusted. The poet-speaker in *State of Siege*, addressing both besiegers and besieged, emphatically states that there "will be no Homeric echo" (184), suggesting that there will be no victor or vanquished in this struggle. Those under siege are aware of the end of heroism, and it is up to the besiegers to understand this now as well.

By deconstructing these motifs (the feminized land, martyrdom, and the quest for heroism) and setting them alongside poetry in which he promoted them, Darwish bolsters the poetic approach he undertook in the last two decades of his life. Resuming the project initiated long ago in the poem "A Soldier Dreams of White Lilies" and in later poems such as "A Canaanite Stone by the Dead Sea," the poet, now much more confrontational, devotes several passages to "a killer" and "a guard," in reference to the Israeli soldiers who thronged his street. The occupiers are barbarians, the poet stresses in *State of Siege*—the only superior quality they possess is "the wisdom of rifles" (197).

Darwish adds that the besiegers are treating their own souls callously and are betraying the suffering of their ancestors in the gas chambers by launching such attacks on those clearly weaker than they (2002, 197). Echoing gestures made in earlier poems, the poet invites the soldiers around his house to share his coffee (186). Then the poet positions himself as teacher to the uncivilized soldier with advanced weapons. By refusing to die "at the gate of [his] deferred death" (236), he offers to teach patience to the soldier who wants to push history along and push the Palestinians out of it. He instructs him on the need for patience as one seeks love "at the entrance to a cafe, your heart slowing down, speeding up" (237). Finally, the poet offers to teach the soldier about the simple fact of their shared humanity and their shared destiny on the same land, assuring him that their estrangement from each other's dining tables will ultimately be brief:

I'll teach you . . .
you have a mother
and I have a mother
and we have the same rain
and we have the same moon
and a short absence from each other's dining tables (238)

Darwish manages to steer the poem to images of ordinary life, and concludes *State of Siege* with a sequence in which he makes incantatory offerings of peace. Without surrendering to sentimentality, the poet describes what is needed for peace as he visualizes this tranquil state:

Peace is to confess the truth publicly:
What have you done to the ghost of those you murdered?

Peace is to take up another task in the garden:
What will we plant next? (2002, 236)

These two stanzas make up a single section and are to be read as one unit. Peace has great potential to bring about the cooperation and advancement of all forms of life in this earthly garden. However, peace requires that one tell the truth about one's crimes, calming the spirits of the dead and the living. The two stanzas of this section stand in confrontation— the white space between them a chasm the aggressor would need to cross for peace to begin. The difference between the two situations, between the judgment of the first question and the reconciliation offered by the next, is stark: in one we imagine a soul in turbulent confrontation with the past, while the other offers us a simple, Edenic vision of the future. And there is no way to peace but through the dark night of the soul, as the lines of poetry containing these two visions refuse to be welded.

In this short lyric, we are indeed inside the Palestinian/ Israeli conflict, and its implications and suffering surround the passage. We witness a mythical moment in which a soul faces a difficult choice that could change the course of its life and that of others. As the poet-speaker dreams of peace, we can begin to imagine that Darwish's words are perhaps inspired by contemporary efforts at peace and reconciliation around the world, an opportunity yet to be offered to his people by their adversaries. We can even imagine these concluding sections of *State of Siege* as a manifesto for conflict resolution that posits poetry as a guide to these difficult, but necessary, undertakings.

State of Siege transforms Palestine from a contentious, incomprehensible part of the world that alternately arouses passions and encourages resignation into a place for continuous and rewarding contemplation of the human condition. As for the poet's own agency, he manages to make a national contingency, after recognizing its historical and traumatic specificity, into a matter from which transcendental lyric can be created. The books following *State of Siege* are also guided by Darwish's stated ambition to be a poet of the absolute—he is convinced that only spiritual and intellectual strength will ensure his and his people's presence on their tenuous ground.

Postscript

Mahmoud Darwish is the last of the twentieth century's world-famous poets, beginning with Tagore and moving on to Hikmet, Pablo Neruda, Faiz Ahmad Faiz, and Nizar Qabbani—poets who drew both popular acclaim and critical attention across national and linguistic borders. The secret of these poets' popularity is both political and musical. Neruda was known for his activism and his championing of the common man. Though he suffered exile and abuse for his political beliefs, Neruda's politics were not what made Neruda a poet. When audiences heard him, they wanted to hear and chant along with *Veinte poemas de amor y una canción desesperada* or *Canto general*, not any of his manifesto poems. Neruda, it should be noted, was a masterful formalist, and his populism went hand in hand with his desire to experiment with new poetic modes and techniques.

Similarly, Tagore represents a separate era in Bengali verse—indeed, in all of India's literatures. Despite being born into an affluent family, he had a strong capacity for humility and empathy that drew various and numerous audiences to him. Writing often from a youthful perspective, Tagore created a level playing field of human emotional expression that made class and caste distinctions dissolve. Tagore innovated and preserved the language of his people; he wrote from within the Bengali tradition and added to it.

Faiz Ahmad Faiz of Pakistan and Nizar Qabbani of Syria were unrequited lovers of other human beings and unrequited seekers of the freedom that eluded them. Echoing and expounding upon the defeats their readers faced on both fronts, the poetry of Faiz and Qabbani attracted rich and poor lovers of Urdu and Arabic poetry, capturing their emotions and channeling them in masterful rhythmic command. They pushed progressive agendas in rhythms that suited the body politic, with emphasis on *body*.

Like them, Darwish, who died in 2008, was a critically acclaimed, traditionally trained, innovative poet who managed to win admirers among those who wanted to preserve traditional poetics and those who called for opening up Arabic verse. He managed to be modern and relevant. The Arab world is full of poets, and very few of them can claim both attributes.

Perhaps harshly but incisively, the Syrian poet Adonis critiqued Darwish for seeking a point of cultural consensus to direct his poetry at. Indeed, Darwish's popularity remains rooted in his early poetry, where his lyrical articulations of Palestinian anger and the desire for emancipation from Israeli oppression met no resistance and struck exactly the right chords among his people and Arabs the world over. Darwish's listeners still recall the freshness of his voice as a discovery of their deep-seated national identity, the poetry giving them a sense of an existential place in the world.

There is no doubt that the enthusiastic and welcoming response Darwish regularly received had impacted him and his sense of what a poet is, or who he was as a poet. The audience's embrace may have limited the range of his tone and positioned him essentially as someone working "from inside the system" of his community's cultural and political machinations. For most of his career, Darwish was affiliated with the Palestinian establishment's institutions, whether formally or informally. Even when assessing his later poems, one cannot say that Darwish directly challenged his culture or was willing to see himself as speaking outside the fold of the We—both Palestinian and Arab. His allusions to religion and Arab patriarchy do not forcefully question the authority of these daunting cultural forces. Less critical of Palestinian and Arab cultural elements than his prose, Darwish's poetry remains largely an articulation of solidarity.

On the other hand, Adonis—Darwish's main contender for prominence among modern Arab poets—saw the poet as both a lifter of the people and a provocateur. In this regard, Adonis feels Darwish fell short since his poetry was a poetry "not of individual confrontational quest, but a poetry of consensus that reflected a collective stance and point of view" (Adonis 2010, 14). According to Adonis, a poet's desire to regenerate a people politically had to be equaled aesthetically (14).

The question remains, however: Can one, in fact, provoke aesthetic regeneration subtly and subversively? And do certain circumstances demand such subtlety? Darwish would definitely argue that his circumstances as a Palestinian dictated such an approach.

In other words, is Darwish's popular acclaim a sign of his weakness as a poet, or is the lack of popular acclaim a failure of poets who never achieved a public platform? What is the point of a deeply revolutionary poem if it is never heard or read? Is poetry contained within the elite capable of affecting a culture, and if so, to what extent? On the other hand, can a poet who does not shake the people's intellectual foundations really challenge them? Is the poet necessarily alienated from society, and does his or her agitated alienation help lead society toward self-criticism? Or is she or he someone who tries to affirm and convince and nudge and steer, but who never leaves the pack? And we may also add, when is each of these "positionings" or a combination of them more appropriate?

The answers to these questions are complicated by the manner in which political stances express themselves aesthetically. Throughout his career, Darwish felt he could not afford to be completely alienated from his people, and influenced as he was by Nizar Qabbani, he was fully aware that the poet's alienation could too easily sound the music of apathy. Early on, Darwish realized that an overly optimistic poetry with a rousing effect has a short fuse and can become a source of bathos rather than pathos. For good or bad, it was Darwish's Palestinianness that kept him from cutting the cord with a badly run national establishment in a cultural setting that was often plagued with intolerance, inconsistency, and lack of discipline. His deep belief in the rightness of his people's claim for their homeland and for self-determination rose above all his criticisms of their culture.

Palestinian culture, like other Arab cultures, may be deeply afflicted with callowness, sexism, and parochialism, but that did not allow Darwish to abandon the Palestinian cause for their land. Nonetheless, from the earliest stages of his career, Darwish sought refuge from the collective spokesmanship that was forced upon him, but that also came to him naturally.

During the relative peace of the Oslo years, when it seemed to Darwish that he had been freed of his political duties, he sought broader horizons. There, too, he chose not to express the bitterness of his exile but tried to seek any sweetness or light that may lie beyond it. This was a fruitful time for him. And even when the al-Aqsa intifada erupted in the fall of 2000, as he joined the ranks expressing the grief of reoccupation, he did so with renewed artistry revealing the reservoirs of dignity and humanity that the Palestinians still held. The occupation did come again, but it found a stronger, wiser Darwish, and the same can be said of his people.

Is Darwish then the last of his kind in his capacity to be the poet of the many, beloved by them, feeling out for them, and feeling in their stead when numbness strikes? He may be. The truth is, Darwish's championing of poets of his own generation was not generous; he *did* like being the prince of Palestinian poets. But by all accounts he was not mean-spirited in his protection of his special status. He supported younger poets in word and by example in an attempt to meld their new poetics into his practice. As the last few chapters of this book have argued, Darwish found great room for agreement with the poets coming after him whose aesthetics were more radical and perhaps more elitist than his.

Though he never took a full dive into free verse, Darwish experimented with it, and his advocacy of it brought readers to new types of poetry who would not have tasted such different approaches without his encouragement (by acting from within). He, in essence, offered his authority as a poet and his credibility as a cultural figure to bridge a public reared on traditional poetics to the new poets who challenged both. Collective solidarity for Darwish went hand in hand with advancing the Palestinians' cause, politically, poetically, and aesthetically. Definitive as he wanted his voice to be, Darwish was intent on not being Palestine's last poet. As it was in the beginning, then, the poet's art feeds his nation in more ways than he and we had ever imagined.

References

Index

References

'Abdulmuṭalib, Muḥammad. 1998. "Taṭwur Tajrubat Maḥmud Darwish al-Shiʻriya." In *Zaitunat al-Manfa; al-ḥalqa al-naqdia fi mahrajan jarashi, 1997*, edited by Jiris Samawi, 77–106. Beirut: Al-mu'assassa al-ʻarabiya lil-dirasat wal-nashr.

Abūbakr, Randah. 1997. "al-Tajrubah al-shakhsiyah ka-taʻabīr 'an waqaʻa ʻām fī shiʻr Dennis Brutus wa *Mahmūd Darwīsh.*" *Alif* (17): 69–98.

Abū Shāwir, Saʻdī. 2003. *Taṭawwur al-ittijāh al-waṭanī fi al-shiʻr al-Filasṭīnī al-muʻāṣir.* Beirut: al-Mu'assasah al-ʻArabīyah lil-Dirāsāt wa-al-Nashr.

Adonis (ʻAli Aḥmad Saʼid). 2010. "Adonis yataḥadath 'an majalat *Shiʻr* wa Maḥmud Darwish wa Najib Maḥfuz." *Al-Hayat*, March 23.

Adorno, Theodor W. 1984. *Aesthetic Theory*. Translated by C. Lenhardt. London: Routledge and Kegan Paul.

al-ʻAili, Anas. "A Plant" in *Ḍuyuf al-nar al-daʼimun: shuʼaraʼ min Filasṭin, 7.* Beirut: al-Mu'assasah al-'Arabiyah lil-Dirasat wa-al-Nashr.

Anderson, Benedict. 2006. *Imagined Communities: Reflections on the Origins and Spread of Nationalism*. London: Verso.

Aristotle. 2007. *Poetics*. Translated by Joe Sachs. Newburyport, MA: Focus Books/R. Pullins Company.

Bailey, John. 2005. *The Power of Delight: A Lifetime in Literature: Essays (1962–2002)*. New York: W. W. Norton.

Bakhtin, Mikhail. 1997. "Al-Khiṭāb fī al-shiʻr wa-al-ḥayāh." In *Madakhil al-shiʻr: Bakhtin, Lautermann, Kondratov*, edited by Amina Rashid and Sayyid Bahrawi. Cairo: Al-Hay'ah al-ʻĀmah li-Quṣur al-Thaqāfah.

Baydūn, ʻAbbās. 1999. "Al-mukhtalif al-ḥaqīqī." In *Mahmūd Darwīsh, al-mukhtalif al-ḥaqīqī: dirāsāt wa-shahādāt*, edited by Samīḥ al-Qāsim et al., 247–49. Amman: Dār al-Shurūq.

Beit-Hallahmi, Benjamin. 1992. *Original Sins: Reflections on the History of Zionism and Israel*. London: Pluto Press.

Bernard-Donals, Michael F. 2009. *Forgetful Memory, Representation and Remembrance in the Wake of the Holocaust*. Binghamton: SUNY Press.

Biale, David. 2010. *Not in the Heavens: The Tradition of Jewish Secular Thought*. Princeton, NJ: Princeton University Press.

Bitton, Simmon. 1997. *Mahmoud Darwich: Et la terre, comme la langue (As the Land Is the Language]* Paris: France 3, Point du Jour. Video recording.

Celik, Ipek Azime. 2008. "Alternative History, Expanding Identity: Myth's Reconsidered in Mahmoud Darwish's Poetry." In *Mahmoud Darwish Exile's Poet: Critical Essays*, edited by Hala Nassar and Najat Rahman, 273–92. Northampton, MA: Olive Branch Press.

Darwish, Mahmoud. 1971. *Shaiʼ ʻan al-waṭan*. Beirut: Dar al-ʼawdah.

———. 1979. *Yawmīyāt al-ḥuzn al-ʻādī*. Beirut: Markaz al-Abḥāth, Munaẓẓamat al-Tahrīr al-Filasṭīnīyah.

———. 1985. "The Madness of Being Palestinian." *Journal of Palestine Studies* 15 (1): 138–41.

———. 1986. *Ward Aquall*. Beirut: Riyyāḍ al-Rāʼyīs lil-Kutub wa-al-Nashr.

———. 1999a. "Al-Hiwār: Maḥmud Darwish . . . La ʻAhad Yaṣil." In *Mahmūd Darwīsh, al-mukhtalif al-ḥaqīqī : dirāsāt wa-shahādāt*, edited by Samīḥ al-Qāsim et al., 13–45. Amman: Dār al-Shurūq.

———. 1999b. "I Discovered That the Earth Was Fragile and the Sea Light." *Boundary 2* 26 (1): 81–83.

———. 2000a. *Adam of Two Edens*. Edited by Munir Akash and Daniel Moore. Syracuse, NY: Syracuse University Press.

———. 2000b. "Palestine: The Imaginary and the Real." In *Innovation in Palestinian Literature: Testimonies of Palestinian Poets and Writers*, revised by Robert Thompson and Izzat Ghazzawi. Translated by Abdul-Fattah Jabr, 15–26. Jerusalem: The NORAD-Ogarit PCP series.

———. 2002. *Ḥalat ḥiṣar*. Beirut: Riyyāḍ al-Rā'yīs lil-Kutub wa-al-Nashr.

———. 2005. *al-'A'māl al-'ulā*. 3 vols. Beirut: Riyyāḍ al-Rā'yīslil-Kutub wa-al-Nashr.

———. 2006. *al-'A'māl al-jadīdah*. Beirut: Riyyāḍ al-Rā'yīs lil-Kutub wa-al-Nashr.

———. 2007a. *Dhākirah lil-nisyān*. Beirut: Riyyāḍ al-Rā'yīs lil-Kutub wa-al-Nashr.

———. 2007b. "Mundu al-'ān 'anta ghairak" (From now on you are not yourself). www.mahmouddarwish.com/ui/english/Show ContentA.aspx?ContentId=26.

Deleuze, Gilles, and Felix Guattari. 1986. *Kafka: Toward a Minor Literature*. Translated by Dana Polan. Minneapolis: University of Minnesota Press.

Ḍuyūf al-nār al-da'imūn: Shu'arā' min falasṭīn. 1999. Beirut: Al-Mu'assasah al-'Arabiya lil-Nashr wal-Tawzia'.

Farsoun, Samih K., and Naseer Hasan Aruri. 2006. *Palestine and the Palestinians: A Social and Political History*. Boulder, CO: Westview Press.

Ganim, Asad. 2001. *The Palestinian-Arab Minority in Israel*. Albany: SUNY Press.

Haddad, Qassim. 2009. "Ta'amulāt min shurfat Mahmūd Darwīsh." Unpublished presentation at the Kennedy Center for the Performing Arts, Washington, D.C., March 10.

al-Ḥāj Ṣāleḥ, Maḥmūd Ibrāhīm. 1999. *Maḥmūd Darwīsh bayna al-zaʿtar wa-al-sabbār: dirāsah naqdiyah.* Damascus: Man-shūrāt Wizārat al-Thaqāfah.

Hall, Stuart. 1994. "Cultural Identity and Diaspora." In *Colonial Discourses and Postcolonial Theory,* edited by P. Williams and L. Chrisman, 392–403. New York: Harvester/Wheatsheaf.

Hall, Stuart, David Morley, and Kuan-Hsing Chen, eds. 1996. *Stuart Hall: Critical Dialogues in Cultural Studies.* London: Routledge.

Harlow, Barbara. 1987. *Resistance Literature.* New York: Methuen.

Hassan, Salah D. 2003. "Nation Validation: Modern Palestinian Literature and the Politics of Appeasement," *Social Text* 21 (2): 7–23.

Hobsbawm, Eric. 1990. *Nations and Nationalism since 1780.* Cambridge: Cambridge University Press.

Ḥussayn, Quṣayy. 1988. *Al-Mawt wal-ḥayāh fī shiʿr al-muqāwamah.* Beirut: Dar Al-Rā'id Al ʿArabī.

Ibrahim, Bashshār. 2005. "Taqdīm." In *Al-tawrātīyāt fī shiʿr Maḥmūd Darwīsh: min al-muqāwamah ilá al-taswiyah,* edited by Aḥmad Ashqar, 7–31. Damascus: Qadmus lil-Nashr wa-al-Tawzīʿ.

Jamal, Amal. 2009. *The Arab Public Sphere in Israel: Media Space and Cultural Resistance.* Bloomington: Indiana University Press.

Jayyusi, Salma Khadra. 1977. *Trends and Movements in Modern Arabic Poetry.* Translated by Christopher Tingley. Amsterdam: Brill.

———. 1992. "Introduction: Palestinian Literature in Modern Times." In *Anthology of Modern Palestinian Literature,* edited by Salma Khadra Jayyusi, 1–80. New York: Columbia University Press.

Kanafani, Ghassan. 1966. *Adab Al-muqawamah fi filasṭin al-muḥtallah.* Beirut: Dar AlAdab.

Kant, Immanuel. 2007. *Critique of Judgment*. New York: Cosimo.

Khalidi, Rashid. 1986. *Under Siege: P.L.O. Decision Making During the 1982 War.* New York: Columbia University Press.

al-Khaṭīb, Yūsuf. 1968. *Dīwān al-waṭan al-muḥtall.* Damascus: Dar Falasṭīn lil-Ta'līf wal-Tarjamah wal-Nashr.

Kimmerling, Baruch. 1999. "Religion, Nationalism and Democracy in Israel." *Constellations* 6 (3): 339–63.

Laidi-Hanieh, Adila, ed. 2008. *Palestine: Rien Ne Nous Manque Ici!* Paris: Editions Cercle.

Laughlin, John Charles Hugh. 2000. *Archeology and the Bible.* London: Routledge.

Mar'i, Sami Khalil. 1978. *Arab Education in Israel.* Syracuse, NY: Syracuse University Press.

Masalha, Nur. 2007. *The Bible and Zionism: Invented Traditions, Archaeology, and Post-colonialism in Israel-Palestine.* London: Zed Books.

Muhawi, Ibrahim. 2006. "Irony and the Poetics of Palestinian Exile." In *Literature and Nation in the Middle East,* edited by Yasir Suleiman and Ibrahim Muhawi, 31–47. Edinburgh: Edinburgh University Press.

Mustafa, Khalid ʿAli. 1978. *Al-Shiʿr al-filisṭini al-ḥadith: 1948–1970.* Baghdad: Manshurat Wizarat al-Thaqafa wa-al-Funun.

al-Nābulusī, Shākir. 1987. *Majnūn al-turāb: dirāsah fī shiʿr wa-fikr Maḥmūd Darwīsh.* Beirut: al-Muʾassasah al-ʿArabīyah lil-Dirāsāt wal-Nashr.

al-Naqqāsh, Rajāʾ. 1971. *Mahmoud Darwish: shāʿir al-arḍ al-muḥtallah.* Cairo: Dār al-Hilāl.

Nāṣir, ʿAlī. 2001. *Bunyat al-qaṣīdah fī shiʿr Maḥmūd Darwīsh.* Beirut: al-Muʾassasah al-ʿArabīyah lil-Dirāsāt wa-al-Nashr.

Nassar, Hala, and Najat Rahman. 2008. "Introduction." In *Mahmoud Darwish Exile's Poet: Critical Essays,* edited by Hala Nassar and Najat Rahman, 1–9. Northampton, MA: Olive Branch Press.

Nasser, Amjad. 1999. "I'tirāf muta'akhir." In *Maḥmūd Darwīsh, al-mukhtalif al- ḥaqīqī: dirāsāt wa-shahādāt*, edited by Samīḥ al-Qāsim et al., 218–21. Amman: Dār al-Shurūq.

Neuwirth, Angelika. 2008. "Hebrew Bible and Arabic Poetry: Mahmoud Darwish's Palestine—From Paradise Lost to a Homeland Made of Words." In *Mahmoud Darwish Exile's Poet: Critical Essays*, edited by Hala Nassar and Najat Rahman, 167–90. Northampton, MA: Olive Branch Press.

Pappe, Ilan. 2011. *The Forgotten Palestinians: A History of the Palestinians in Israel*. New Haven, CT: Yale University Press.

Qabbani, Nizar. *Shuʻarāʼ al-arḍ al-muḥtallah—al-Quds*. Beirut: Manshurat Nizar Qabbani, 1968.

Qahwajī, Ḥabīb. 1972. *Al-ʻArab fī ẓill al-iḥtilāl al-ʼisrāʼīlī (1948– 1967)*. Beirut: Markaz al-ʼAbḥathh al-Ṭibāʻah li-Munaẓamat al-Tahrīr al-Falasṭīniyah.

al-Qaissī, Yaḥyá. 2008. September 20–21. "Min ḥayāt Darwish fī ʻAmmān." *Al-Quds al-ʻarabī* newspaper, "Mulḥaq Khaṣ" (special supplement on Mahmoud Darwish), 9–11.

al-Rifaʻi, Jamāl Aḥmād. 1994. *Athar al-thaqāfa al-ʻibriyāh fi al-shiʻr al-falasṭini: Dirāsa fi shiʻr Maḥmūd Darwīsh*. Cairo: Dar al-thaqafa al-jadida.

Said, Edward. 1999. *After the Last Sky* (with photographs by Jean Mohr). 2nd ed. New York: Columbia University Press.

———. 2004. "Thoughts on Late Style." *London Review of Books*, August 5.

Saleḥ, Fakhri. 1999. "Maḥmūd Darwīsh: sinaʻāt al-usṭura al-filas-ṭiniya" In *Maḥmūd Darwīsh, al-mukhtalif al-ḥaqīqī : dirāsāt wa-shahādāt*, 35–54. Amman: Dār al-Shurūq.

al-Sayyid, Nāẓim. 2008. September 20–21. "Maḥmūd Darwīsh fī khaymatihi al-Beirūtiyah," *Al-Quds Al-ʻarabī* newspaper, "Mulḥaq khaṣ" (special supplement on Mahmoud Darwish), 6–8.

Schultz, Helena Lindholm, with Julianne Hammer. 2003. *The Palestinian Diaspora: Formation of Identities and Politics of Homeland*. London: Routledge.

Segal, Hanna. 1998. "A Psychoanalytic Approach to Esthetics." In *Reading Melanie Klein*, edited by John Phillips and Lyndsey Stonebridge, 199–218. London: Routledge.

al-Shaikh, Abdul-Rahim. 2006. "Fleeting Heterotopias: Troy, Andalusia, and the Whirling Darwish of Palestine." Unpublished paper presented at the Humanities Conference, University of Carthage, July 3–7.

———. 2009. "Palästina: Leben im Tunnel." In *Di/Visions—Kultur und Politik des Nahen Ostens*, edited by Catherine David, Georges Khalil, and Bernd M. Scherer, 191–214. Goettingen: Wallstein Verlag.

Shalat, Antoine. 1999. "'Ala jabhat al-sirā' ma'a al-thaqāfah al-'isrā'īliyah: Maḥmūd Darwīsh wa dalat al-ḥajah 'ila al-ḥiwār." In *Maḥmud Darwīsh: al-mukhtalif al-ḥaqīqī*, 145–62. Ramallah: Dar al-Shuruq.

Shihade, Magid. 2011. *Not Just a Soccer Game: Colonialism and Conflict Among Palestinians in Israel*. Syracuse, NY: Syracuse University Press.

Shklovsky, Victor. 1988. "Art as Technique." In *Modern Criticism and Theory: A Reader*, edited by David Lodge, 16–30. Translated by Lee T. Lemon and Marion J. Reis. London: Longmans.

Shryock, Andrew. 2004. "The New Jordanian Hospitality: House, Host, and the Guest in the Culture of Public Display." *Comparative Studies in Society and History* 46 (1): 35–62.

Smooha, Sammy. 1989. *Arabs and Jews in Israel: Conflicting and Shared Attitudes in a Divided Society*. Boulder, CO: Westview Press.

Snir, Reuven. 2008. "'Other Barbarians Will Come': Intertextuality, Meta-Poetry, and Meta-Myth in Mahmoud Darwish's Poetry." In *Mahmoud Darwish Exile's Poet: Critical Essays,* edited by Hala Nassar and Najat Rahman. Northampton, MA: Olive Branch Press.

Spivak, Gayatri Chakravorty. 1993. *Outside in the Teaching Machine*. New York: Routledge.

———. 1999. *A Critique of Postcolonial Reason: Toward a History of the Vanishing Present*. Cambridge, MA: Harvard University Press.

Sulaiman, Khalid A. 1984. *Palestine and Modern Arab Poetry*. London: Zed Books.

Todorov, Tzvetan. 1984. *Mikhail Bakhtin: The Dialogical Principle*. Translated by Wlad Godzich. Minneapolis: University of Minnesota Press.

al-'Ustā, 'Ādil. 2001. *'Arḍ al-qaṣīdah: jidāriyat: Maḥmud Darwīsh wa silatahu bi-'asha'ārihi*. Ramallah: Dar Al-Zahrah lil-Nashr wa-al-Tawzi', Bait Al-Shi'r.

Wāzin, 'Abduh. 2006. *Maḥmūd Darwīsh al-gharīb yaqa' 'alá nafsih: qirā'ah fī a'mālih al-jadīdah*. Beirut: Riad Rayyes Books.

Wiesel, Elie. 1990. "The Holocaust as Literary Inspiration." In *Dimensions of the Holocaust: Lectures at Northwestern University*, 2nd ed., annotated by Elliott Lefkowitz, 5–19. Evanston, IL: Northwestern University Press.

Yaḥyá, Aḥlām. 2003. *'Awdat al-hiṣān al-ḍā'i': waqfah qaṣīrah ma'a al-shā'ir Maḥmud Darwish : dirāsah naqdīyah*. Damascus: Nīnawá lil-Dirāsāt wa-al-Nashr wa-al-Tawzī'.

Zaqtan, Ghassan. 1999. "'Akthhāriyāt al-hāmish." In *Ḍuyūf al-nār al-dā'imūn: shu'arā' min Filasṭīn*, 135–36. Beirut: al-Mu'assasah al-'Arabīyah lil-Dirāsāt wa-al-Nashr.

Index